the
Last night

**A CAREGIVER'S JOURNEY THROUGH
TRANSITION AND BEYOND**

A CAREGIVER'S JOURNEY THROUGH TRANSITION AND BEYOND

BERNNADETTE STANIS

JAED PUBLICATIONS
Los Angeles, California

JAED PUBLICATIONS
Los Angeles, California

Copyright @ May 2016 by BernNadette Stanis

ISBN 978-0-9976552-0-9

Instagram: Thelmaofgoodtimes

Twitter: Thelmagoodtimes

Publisher Website: jaedpublications.com

Printed at OneTouchpoint-Southwest in Austin, Texas, United States of America

DEDICATION

This book is dedicated to my mother Eula Stanislaus and to all the wonderful people we have met along our journey through Alzheimer's, and to those who were there to help us in our darkest hours, you have my love forever.

ACKNOWLEDGMENTS

A special thanks to all of the pastors across this nation who have been there to support my cause to fight Alzheimer's, thank you for the wonderful words of encouragement that meant so much to me. To the politicians who have helped me bring awareness of this disease to the forefront, thank you. To the educators in the medical field who have continuously educated me on the progression of this disease, and who have given me the information on how to be healthy in our world today, thank you. To all my fans that have remained true and supportive of me throughout my career and to my siblings, I sincerely thank you.

THE SERENITY PRAYER

God grant me the serenity to accept the things
I cannot change;
Courage to change the things that I can;
And Wisdom to know the difference.
Living one day at a time...
Enjoying one moment at a time Accepting hardships as the
pathway to Peace;
Taking as He did this sinful world as it is;
not as I would have it.
Trusting that He will make all things right
if I surrender to His Will;
That I may be reasonably happy in this life
And supremely happy with Him
Forever in the next. Amen.

– Anonymous

MY PRAYER

Let me be the vessel to write the Truth,
To write the Real,
There are so many people who need to Heal.
Thank You My Father Lord and Savior,
That as I write on these pages
Those who may read them would excuse
The water marks from my tears.
I am writing from the deepest part of me.
My soul, my soul, my lonely emptiness.
But I am full of Love for all who may be here now,
Or who may be here one day.
"I Love You"
Just to hear those words
At certain times in our lives
When we are hurting
Can help us through
"I Love You"

by BernNadette Stanis

PROLOGUE

The personal journey I will share with you in the pages of this story is about the relationship I shared with my mom through her struggle with Alzheimer's and our everyday living with this devastating disease. Alzheimer's not only affects the person who has been diagnosed with it, but their family members, especially the caregiver. I was my mom's caregiver.

The failure to find a cure for this disease is the true horror of Alzheimer's. Medical researchers and scientists have no explanation why it attacks the minds of those who are intelligent, contributing members of society. There are millions of people living with Alzheimer's, and when you consider family and friends, the disease affects a much larger number of people. Because of the amount of destruction the disease can cause, Alzheimer's has a devastating affect, robbing the victim of one of life's most precious gifts, their memory. It is a wild beast that sets itself within the fibers of one's brain cells and takes up residence there. Once it settles in, there is no removing it. It is there to stay and do its inevitably fatal job. I will always call this disease the "monster of the mind." It is more vicious than any invasion known to man.

I watched as my mother slowly disappeared out of my life. My shattered, broken heart splintered into pieces with every stage of this monster. Although this was a very difficult book to write, it was one that I knew had to be written. I strongly feel this is a book Mom really wanted me to write for you, as well. Although there are many books written on Alzheimer's, there was none I would refer to as my friend or companion. I only wished there had been a book like this available for me when Mom and I struggled through our darkest hours. I call this book my companion book for caregivers. I wrote it so it can become your friend, a friend who understands your pain, hurt, and lonely tears that fall in the middle of the night.

I also wrote this book because maybe someone who is a caregiver right now will not feel as I did, lost and afraid, with nowhere to run and escape. There are places on the Internet where someone can read about the stages of the disease, but they can never explain the pain of what it is to live with and be a part of Alzheimer's every day until this monster has done its job. It was a very lonely place for me. I can tell the story of how Mom suffered from Alzheimer's, but cannot find the words to describe the pain in my heart.

I prayed that God would help me find a cure to save Mom's life. I just couldn't believe there wasn't a cure or an answer to this monster. Every day I searched and prayed. I took Mom to doctor after doctor; we tried different foods, vitamins and medicines. Nothing really helped; it slowed the disease but there was no cure. I finally had to accept our fate. I decided to make everyday a special one for Mom. I danced with her, played all of her favorite music and talked about her high school days. I did everything that I thought would make her happy.

In life there are situations that will arise to challenge us, and we must know that we are bigger than the fears that engulf us during these crisis. I had to endure the fear of what Alzheimer's did to Mom and deal with the pain it left in my heart. I did not know or understand this disease that had so abusively grabbed hold of Mom, and me as her caregiver. I shook and fought, cried and pleaded for it to let us go. But its ugly claws became deeply set in and would never release us. I know this book will help someone, somewhere, to hold on through an awful time in his or her life. It is helping me right now, even though I am the writer.

This is not an autobiography, but a look at part of my story for now. It is also about my parents, grandparents, and siblings. I will write about some of the fun times and wonderful lessons I learned throughout my life with Mom and Dad, and some wonderful times with my four siblings. I will also share with the reader, the many different roads we faced with twists and turns, and how it all played out in an American family's life; a family from the Brownsville section of Brooklyn, New York.

I want you to get to know who my parents were as individuals. I want you to appreciate their lives and what they endured, accomplished, and enjoyed in the time I had them here on earth. I will share with you the part that hurts the most; losing my dear, sweet mother to the dreaded monster of the mind disease, and losing my beloved father to the ugly, cold, viciousness of violence.

Most important, this story is about my mother's walk through a dark valley, with her daughter's hand to hold as her only light at times. You will read how my mother, through her darkest hours, taught her most profound lessons. You will know how the blessings of God remained with her to the very end of her life. I've learned so much from her sweet, gentle spirit. It meant the world to me when she spoke, and although her words became fewer and fewer as the disease progressed, every word she uttered came from a special love and truth deep in her heart.

My one constant prayer during this time was that Mom and I would never lose our connection to one another. I prayed that God would always let her know me and be able to communicate with me. My prayer was answered and we communicated together when words were not necessary. We truly possessed a special bond throughout our lives as mother and daughter.

This book's name reflects the last night my mother and I had together at the hospital. It was the most beautiful, peaceful, God-filled night that I have ever experienced. That night taught me what we refer to as death should be called transcending; the understanding that when we move to a higher ground, the Angels of God are all around us. God was there in the room with us and I could see and feel Mom at one with the Lord. She had always been brave, fearless and very strong, throughout her life. Why would it be any different at death?

I chose to write *The Last Night*, celebrating fond memories of Mom's life that she shared with those she loved the most; her parents, her husband, her children and grandchildren. I will take you down memory lane, telling her story the way she would have told it if Alzheimer's had not taken over and destroyed those very memories she most enjoyed.

The ultimate purpose of this book is, once you read it you will know who this incredible woman, daughter, mother, wife and beautiful spiritual human being was before, during and at the end of Alzheimer's. I sincerely want you to clearly understand her importance to me as her daughter, and feel our love and how I honored her as my mother. Please allow these words on these pages to speak to your heart, as it has spoken to mine

1.

MEET MY GRANDPARENTS
LOUISE AND WILBERT (MOM'S PARENTS)
BEATRICE AND SIMEON (DAD'S PARENTS)
AND MY PARENTS
GREGORY AND EULA

My mother, Eula Stansilaus, was born in Jeanerette, Louisiana on September 30, 1931 to sixteen-year-old Louise Boutee and twenty-two- year old Wilbert James. Young people married early back in those days and my grandparents were no exception. Jeanerette was known as the "Sugar City" because of the cane fields, refineries and sugar mills in the town.

Mom was her parent's only child and they lavished her with love and affection. I remember Mom telling me stories of her childhood. She had an amazing memory and could recall things as far back as when she was only two years old.

"Can you remember this, Bern?" she asked me once while telling me one of my favorite stories of her childhood. "I had to sleep between my parents with Mom on my right side and Dad on my left. If I put my leg on one parent, I'd have to put my other leg on the other one."

She did this because she always wanted to be fair, and not show more love to one parent over the other. When she told me that story, it didn't surprise me because that was how she treated all five of her children, generous and fair. She shared so much affection with us, we knew that we were loved.

"You had to be fair like that because you are a Libra and the scales always have to balance," I joked with her.

She laughed. "Yeah, maybe that's the reason."

She shared more stories about her childhood with me. At dinner time in their home, Mom would sit at the table next to her dad and eat out of his plate, but her mother did not allow her daughter to do the same with her.

"No, Eula, this is my plate and that's you and Daddy's plate over there," she would say. Grandma always laughed at them both eating out of one plate but she also really loved how close they were.

Mom had nothing but good memories for the first five years of her life. She especially recalled riding her shiny, red tricycle she received on her third birthday. She rode that bike all day until the sun went down. She also recalled the joy she found playing with her cousin. But that abruptly ended when her parents decided to move to Texas.

In Louisiana, they had lived with her grandmother and when her parents decided to relocate to Texas my great-grandmother, Cora Mac Boutee (or just mama as we called her), suggested that they leave my mother with her. She argued that would free her parents of the chore to raise a small child and they could focus on getting settled in their new home.

"No, Mama, I'm taking my little Eula with me," my grandmother told her mother.

Grandmother was confident that she and her husband would be fine. My grandfather had been offered a position as a chauffeur which assured him of a steady paycheck. Grandmother had worked for a very wealthy white woman named Miss Emily in Louisiana. Because of the many skills she learned from Miss Emily, Grandmother also felt confident she could find employment.

Louise was one of ten children, six girls and four boys. She was forced to leave school in the fifth grade to financially help the family. That is when she went to work for Miss Emily. She was only ten years old when she began working for the lady. During her long tenure with Miss Emily, the lady taught Grandmother how to prepare some very outstanding dishes. Later in life, she became an outstanding cook which served her well when she moved to Texas.

Grandmother's education with Miss Emily began one day when she was giving the older lady a bath. Grandmother was having a very difficult time holding Miss Emily up to help her get into the tub because she was rather small. The overweight woman slipped from Grandmother's grip.

"Fe Pe Tae," the lady shouted at my grandmother, which was another name for a female dog.

"No, you're fe pe tae," Grandmother said back to Miss Emily, having no idea what the word meant and stumbling over the pronunciation.

Miss Emily broke out into a raucous laugh. "You're a spicy one," she said. "And if you're going to say the word, then say it right." That began my grandmother's lessons in Patois French.

As Grandmother grew into a young girl, Miss Emily gave her some very beautiful clothes that she was allowed to wear to church on Sundays. Every other Sunday Grandmother would switch clothes with her sister so that she could go to church in pretty clothes also.

Miss Emily became quite attached to Grandmother and trusted that she would never leave her. She stayed with Miss Emily as long as she could—for ten years. When Grandmother married, Miss Emily didn't want her to leave, and when she was pregnant with and gave birth to my mom, the old lady still did not want her to leave. Finally the day came when Grandmother told Miss Emily that she had decided to move to Texas. It was a very sad day for the two of them.

Grandmother had grown to love Miss Emily. She had taught her so many useful things that would eventually help her through life. Not only did my grandmother learn to speak and understand French and become an awesome cook, she learned the value of beautiful fine antiques, paintings, china and crystal. Working for Miss Emily was a blessing for my grandmother as much as it was for Miss Emily.

Grandmother always said, "That white woman treated me like a daughter."

Miss Emily eventually gave my grandmother many of her fine treasured belongings. "I want you to have them because I know you will take care of them, Louise," she said.

Grandmother did take care of them and continued to always talk about Miss Emily the rest of her life. Mom told me how Grandmother cried the day she left the old lady to go out into the world to begin her own life. Grandmother stayed with Emily until one of her family members from up north came to care for her. I don't think my grandmother ever saw Miss Emily after that day. When she left Jeanerette, she did not return for many years.

Relocating from Jeanerette to Houston turned out to be a major move for my grandparents. My grandmother, being an excellent cook, brought in lots of money for the family, and along with my grandfather's salary they did quite well. They were happy and successful, but after one year in Texas, Grandmother decided she wanted to move to New York.

She was still a very young woman, now twenty-one, and she desired a little more out of life.

My grandfather, being very much stuck in his ways, did not want to leave Texas. He told grandmother she could go and take my mother with her. If she didn't like New York, she could always come back home and they would build a restaurant for her and call it Louise's Lounge. It appeared that Grandfather loved his wife very much and wanted her to be happy.

As a young girl, Mom had mixed emotions about leaving Texas. Her mother had told her great stories about New York and showed her pictures depicting the beauty of the city. Her excitement, however, was curtailed when she found out that her dad would not be going with them. Mom asked her dad to please come with them.

Her dad smiled and said, "You'll be fine, baby. I'll come up to visit you all the time and if you don't like it there you can always come back home and live here with me."

Mom accepted her dad's promise to come and see them in New York. She felt satisfied as they prepared to leave. But that satisfaction dissipated as she walked down the driveway and got into the backseat of the car that would take them to the train station, and saw her red tricycle her dad had purchased after they moved to Texas. She pleaded with her mother to take the tricycle. But her mom responded.

"No, Eula, we can't take it with us baby. We're going to have to leave it behind. We just don't have enough room."

For the first time, I believe Mom experienced the feeling of separation and loss, having to leave her dad and her treasured tricycle. But as much as she loved her dad and her tricycle, Mom exhibited at an early age certain strength of character. She quickly recovered from her hurt so the feeling of separation and loss was only temporary. Her dad promised to come and visit them in New York, and just as she got a new bike in Houston she knew she would also get a new one in her new home.

One of my grandmother's close friends from Texas, Corine, who eventually became my godmother, had moved to New York a year before they did. She'd settled in Brooklyn and was doing quite well. When Mom and Grandmother arrived in New York, Corrine moved them in with her. They stayed there for a couple months, then Grandmother found a job and they moved into their own apartment, also in Brooklyn.

One of the first things that Grandmother did after moving was look for a school for Mom to attend that September, and she found P.S. 28, right near her new place in Brooklyn. Education was very important to my grandmother.

My grandmother was one of ten children; six girls and four boys. She left school in the fifth grade to help out her family. When she went to work for Miss Emily she was ten years old. My grandmother was very smart and it really hurt her to have to leave school at such an early age. She wanted to become a teacher, but her family's financial needs prevented that from happening. I believe that is why my grandmother stressed the importance of an education for my mother.

Mom told me that she and her mother had a close relationship and her mother always told her "This is what I want for you Eula: I want you to go to school and become well-educated, and to be a good girl until you get married." Now "good girl" in those days meant being a virgin until marriage. Mom promised her mother that she would honor all of her wishes, and it made my grandmother so proud of her daughter.

Mom's passion growing up was going to the movies and keeping scrapbooks of the stars that she most admired. Mom and Grandma would go to see all of the Shirley Temple movies. When Mom was twelve years old, she went to see the movie National Velvet, starring Elizabeth Taylor, the young beautiful actress who was taking over Hollywood. Mom loved Ms. Taylor and she also loved Lena Horne. All the young Black girls especially wanted to be like Ms. Horne. A few years later, Mom attended Girls' High School, the same school that her idol had attended years before. At least in that way, she got her wish to be like Lena Horne, the woman she looked up to.

The actress, Roxy Roker, who played the upstairs neighbor, Helen White on the television show, *The Jeffersons*, also went to Girls' High School. While taping an episode for *Good Times*, on the CBS lot, this extremely nice, pretty lady came over to me and said.

"I know your mother. Your mother's name is Eula, right?"

"Yes," I said with a surprised look on my face. I wondered how she knew Mom.

"I was your mom's big sister at Girls' High," Roxy said. "When a new freshman class came into the school," she continued, "each of the senior girls had to pick out a freshman to be her big sister. The big sister helped the freshman get used to the transition to high school and was there for them if they needed help with their school work."

I smiled and gave her Mom's phone number at home, and she also gave me her number for Mom. They called each other several times after that and I'm sure they both had a lot in common because Ms. Roker's son, Lenny Kravits, also became a famous entertainer.

Mom formed a lot of friendships in high school. She told us about "those wonderful days," as she called them, when her friends would come over to her house on Friday nights and they'd listen to music, dance and play cards until late into the night. Grandmother would be in the kitchen all the time making good old gumbo, along with her many other Louisiana dishes for them.

A few of Mom's friends called her "Tex" late into her teen years. When she told me of that nickname I naturally wondered why.

"Because when I first moved to New York," she explained. "My mom would dress me in these cute, short dresses with two long braids on each side of my head. My hair was very long, down to the middle of my back, and the kids thought that I had a Texas accent. That's why the nickname stuck with me. They called me 'Tex' and I answered to the name."

We both smiled and got a good laugh. She said, "Yeah that's what they called me."

Mom loved New York because it was an exciting place to live. But she still missed her dad. She wrote him letters every week and visited him for a week in the summers. Grandpa would send Mom money to buy clothes and often sent her greeting cards with money tucked inside. Grandma also bought Mom lots of pretty and modern clothes along with beautiful shoes. Mom was so well-dressed that her classmates voted her "Best Dressed at Girls' High School."

When Mom turned sixteen, Grandma gave her a Sweet Sixteen Birthday Party. One of her friends asked her what she would like as a birthday present.

"I would like a rosary," Mom said.

Her friend took Mom to buy a rosary and she picked out a beautiful silver one. She kept that rosary her entire life. I remember seeing it often when I was a little girl. One time I asked Mom why she asked for a rosary. She told me it was because she loved the Blessed Virgin Mary, but also because when she was fourteen, she had gone to see the movie, *The Song of Bernadette*. She loved the movie so much that she said right then, "If I ever have a daughter, I'm going to name her Bernadette." That's how I got my name.

I can remember all my life Mom would always say, "Don't forget where your name came from. It's a blessed name, Bern."

Grandma was doing well in New York selling her special Louisiana-style dinners and giving her famous card parties on weekends. She had no plans to return to Texas. She and Mom were happy but Grandmother did reach out to Grandfather and asked him to join them in New York. But he was just as content living in Texas and decided to stay there. Eventually, Grandma stopped asking him and she finally realized that they would never be a family again. She was right. My grandparents eventually divorced and both finally remarried.

When Mom turned sixteen years old, Grandma allowed her to date. But she was really a shy girl and if left to find someone to date probably would have missed out. But her girlfriend, Annie Carrol, would not allow that to happen. One day Annie came to visit Mom with her boyfriend and another friend, Gregory Talbert Stanislaus. Mom was instantly struck with the young man's good looks.

"Greg had great features," she told me with a smile. "He had a nice nose; it was so straight and perfect. His complexion was an olive color and his hair was Indian straight with a little wave to it."

He stood a little shorter than what Mom liked, but at five-foot-nine-and-a-half inches, his good looks and confidence made him appear well over six-feet. His great personality made him even taller than that. Needless to say, he won Mom over.

Gregory Talbert Stanislaus was not just a handsome man, but a man with great morals, high standards and ideals, thanks to his parents who were both from the West Indies. His father, Simeon James Stanislaus was a tall man of great stature. Grandfather stood over six-feet-two-inches and had a muscular body. Dad's mother, Beatrice Patrice, was a tiny woman only four-feet-eleven-inches tall. She had bone straight hair like an Italian.

They both came from Carriacou, a small island off the coast of Grenada. It had the reputation of being the friendliest, healthiest and safest island in the Caribbean. Simeon hailed from Bellevue, South Carriacou and Beatrice from Windward, Carriacou. They married there in the West Indies and had their first child, a son named Cassian. A few years later, Simeon got a job in the United States working on the Holland Tunnel. He brought his wife and child to the States and my father, Gregory, was born on Warren Street in Brooklyn. Soon after, a daughter Edith was born.

My grandmother Beatrice began to miss her family in the West Indies and wanted to return home. My grandfather remained in the States working while she went back to the West Indies with her three children. But he traveled back and forth to see his family.

Reflecting back on my dad's parents, I can remember Grandpa Simeon was a very nice, kind and gentle man, always appeared to be happy and easy going. When I would go over to his home, a nice brownstone in Brooklyn, Grandpa would usually be sitting at his window in a big green chair with a pillow to support his back. It seemed like the world revolved around him because we all would gather in the room, while he sat in his chair, and talk and just have fun.

My Aunt Edith, Dad's sister was very close to Grandpa Simeon. She was truly a daddy's girl. Aunt Edith and my dad managed Grandpa Simeon's few apartment buildings he owned in Brooklyn. We all deeply loved Grandpa Simeon. Thinking of him now always brings a smile to my face. My time with him was much too short. I was seven years old when he passed away from a heart attack.

Dad's mom Beatrice remained in the West Indies most of her life. I was ten years old when she came back to the United States to visit with us one summer. All I knew about Grandmother was exactly what Dad told me. She was a small but strong-willed woman. She did not take any mess from anyone. Dad told me that she was a disciplinarian, who taught him self-respect and dignity, values that she insisted that her children follow at all times. Dad loved and respected his mother and that love showed throughout his life.

Grandmother Beatrice had a beautiful voice and sang and danced. Her talent was very visible when she came to visit us that one summer. I was so excited because it would be the first time I met her. My biggest surprise when I first saw her was her size. She was 4'11" and weighed 105 pounds, exactly my size. I couldn't stop just staring at her because she was so cute. I was most amazed by the way she carried her purse, or back then we called it a pocket book. She put the straps on her shoulder, the same way they carry purses today. Back then no one put their straps on their shoulders; they always put it on their arm. She would fit right in today, carrying it that way.

It was during that summer that I learned so much about my dad and his mom. I sat in the living room and watched the two of them together. I had never seen him with his mother before. He looked so happy and I guess that's the way he was as a kid in the West Indies. They really looked so cute together and looked just alike. Every day Dad would play his saxophone and Grandma would sing all of the songs she taught him as a boy. They sounded wonderful together. The two of them appeared so happy and I will forever hold that memory of them enjoying their good old days.

When Dad turned eighteen years old, he returned to the United States. Having been born in New York, he was an American citizen. He joined the Army and served four years before getting an Honorable Discharge. After leaving the Army, he moved in with his father in Brooklyn and enrolled in music school. He trained on the saxophone and also became a composer. He played in bands around New York and other cities across the country. Dad would play for Mom and my grandmother. After he and Mom married, she knew almost as much as he did about music, and all the great singers and musicians of that time.

One time I asked Dad about his initial impression of Mom when he first saw her that day with his friends. He said she was beautiful, with a fantastic figure. Mom's measurements were 34-24-36, and she stood five-feet-six-inches tall and weighed 128 pounds. She had long hair that flowed almost to her waist and relished a beautiful smile.

"What wasn't there to like?" he asked with a smile.

After that first meeting, Dad would stop by to see his girl just to say hello every single day for the next four years. Being seven years older than Mom, he knew that he would have to wait until she was older to ask for her hand in marriage. Until then, they went out to parties at his family's house and they double dated with friends. They loved to go bowling and play board games. But they most enjoyed the weekend parties that my grandmother gave. The great dinners and the card games were their favorite activities back then.

Dad told me that his father advised him, "If you have to pick a wife, you must pick Eula because she is the best one for you."

He followed his father's advice and proposed to Mom when she turned nineteen years old and they married when she turned twenty. They had a big engagement party with all of their family and friends there to celebrate the occasion.

Mom and Dad got married on a beautiful June day at Saint Peter Claver's Catholic Church in Brooklyn. Mom had kept her promise to her mother to be well-educated, lady like, and a "good girl" and Grandmother gave her a wedding ceremony fit for a fairy-tale princess. My grandfather came to New York for his little girl's wedding. My parents had the reception at the St. George Hotel in Brooklyn and the newlyweds went to Niagara Falls for their honeymoon.

2.

I was the first child born to Eula and Greg Stanislaus. Mom named me Bernadette just as she said she would. Mom and Dad had four other children, Gregory Kyle, Talbert Kethrell (Trell), Deborah Louise and Yolanda Stanislaus. We grew up in the Van Dykes Projects in the Brownsville section of Brooklyn. It was one of the worst sections of the city and we were exposed to a lot of things living in this area. Despite our surroundings, my parents were determined to do their best for their five children; this was paramount to them, even though they faced many challenges doing so.

We went to Our Lady of Loretto, a parochial school ten blocks away from home and on our way to school I remember seeing heroin addicts. They would be so high and would always do the same slow nod, bending their knees until they were about an inch or two from the ground. The kids used to make bets on which addict would hit the ground first. But they would never fall, and would always prop back up. It was an amazing sight, seeing junkies with their swollen hands in a frozen position, hands twice their normal size from all the needles being inserted into their veins.

My father told us that he could have taken his money and bought a big house somewhere in the suburbs like many of his friends did, but he and Mom decided to invest their money in the children. Both of them stressed the importance of a good education for our future. And Dad also encouraged us in the arts. He loved music and dancing all of his life, and I believe the talent that we have as his children came straight from my dad's mother, Beatrice.

Grandmother Beatrice was a beautiful and talented woman who could sing and was a singer and dancer in her home town. Dad said she always encouraged him to sing with her and eventually they did shows together.

"If there are two stars in this place, I know I am one," Grandmother once told my dad when they were at a party.

Having children who were inclined to the arts—music, dance, and singing—had to be demanding on my parents. But somehow they managed to put all five of us through parochial school as well as put us in our dance, music and singing classes.

My parents just didn't invest their money, they invested time in all five of us. They had a vision and a dream; both wanted to give their children the best opportunity in life so that we would ultimately become successful adults. It made us a very busy bunch of kids, something good in more ways than one. For starters, being busy kept us out of trouble. My parents always knew where each one of us were, at all times. Believe me, we were too busy to have time for anything but getting through school and practicing our arts. It seems that my parents had us active every hour of the day, and I think that was by design so that we were too occupied for any kind of nonsense. Smart plan, huh?

Mom was both a calming force and the wind beneath our wings. She showed us a lot of love along with patience and understanding. She spoke to us in that sweet, quiet voice of hers that gave us a feeling of security and confidence. But believe me, as Dad used to say, Mom was "no joke." He was right. Mommy was always so cool, but she would never tolerate any disrespect from her children.

I can remember many times when we were little kids, if we were being bad and Mom would give us a spanking, she just calmly sat in her chair and without raising her voice called out our name and said.

"Come over here and lay across my lap right now."

Can you imagine a kid walking to their own spanking? Well, that's what we had to do, walk over there and lay across her lap. She would then give us two or three smacks on the butt, and they would hurt. Then she would say.

"Okay, get up and go sit down."

As I think back about that today, she had some kind of control over her kids because none of us would run away from the whipping we were about to get. I always thought that was amazing; she never had to run after us or yell and lose her composure. She was not having that.

Mom and Dad worked closely together when it came to raising us. They made us show respect to them and others. For example, if we asked Dad if we could do something, he would ask us, "What did your mother say?" It was always Mom's decision if we did something or went somewhere or not. Mom would never let us disrespect Dad's house rules either, and when he set the rules, we followed them. He was the boss.

I can remember the advice Dad used to give us growing up. He instilled in us, from the time we were small children that with education behind us and determination within us, there was no place in the world we couldn't go.

"With a good education and determination you can attain any goal in life you set for yourself," he would say.

My dad was wise and made sure he daily shared his wisdom with us. I still hear his words in my head and my heart every single day of my life. He would say to us, "Keep your nose clean;" "Don't take wooden nickels;" and "What's for you is for you and no one can take it from you." But his most famous saying, the one we heard most often was. "What's around you does not have to be in you."

Even though our neighborhood had a lot of rough edges, such as drug use and gangs, we didn't have to participate in that craziness. My parents were not playing with us when it came to things like staying out of trouble, and respecting ourselves and our family name. They would never tolerate any of us getting involved with that negative stuff. I am proud to say that not one of their children has ever done drugs. And that is a big deal for having children who grew up in the 1970's when drugs were as big as they are today, maybe even bigger. The advice from our parents and the way they explained life to us, with honesty and love, is one of the reasons why we stayed focused and on the right path through the hard times we experienced in our lives.

Growing up, Brownsville was a wonderful experience for us children. It was where our friends also lived and where we felt love all around us. Many people may not understand why we had such strong feelings living in a tough neighborhood, but life was much different back then. No matter what people saw on the outside, viewing our world from within, you found a lot of love and friendship. My parents sheltered us from the harshness of our surroundings by encouraging us to dream about a world of possibilities, one without limits.

We believed we could accomplish whatever we set as our goals. I am so thankful that they raised us that way. As children, when you have that kind of outlook, it allows you to dream without fear, so when you become an adult and encounter some of the limitations in the world, you won't buy into it at all. But our dreams were always accompanied by hard work, discipline and a healthy dose of self-esteem.

Mom was the support that encouraged us through it all. Somehow she always saw the good in things. But on the other hand, if something was bad she could see it coming from a mile away and would guide us away from it. Without complaining, Mom steered the ship through the rocky waters of life and held it together, along with us.

Dad was more of an activist, seeking justice for all people. He couldn't stand to see anyone treated unfairly. He was called a true activist of his time from those who knew him. One of his mottoes was "help somebody." He worked with Shirley Chisholm and other leaders of the community to help make life better. He worked in public housing as a Resident Coordinator, assisting the residents find jobs and better housing.

One of my most vivid memories of Dad came when I was about three or four years old. It's amazing what you can remember from that age. Dad would go to his band rehearsals and I always wanted to go with him, and he would take me. I recall just how fast he walked and I had to constantly jog to keep up with him. At rehearsal I loved watching the band play all sorts of songs. I especially loved when they played West Indian music, and of course I just danced away. Dancing has always been in my bones and I did it all the time to all sorts of music. To dance meant to be free with no limits. I guess you can say I was born to dance.

I still love the sound of the saxophone, even to this day. I'm sure it's because of those early days at Dad's rehearsals. My father was just awesome on the alto saxophone. He read music as fast as he read the newspaper. There was always music and dancing in our family. Even though Mom wasn't West Indian, she loved to do the Calypso dances. And Dad always sang the musical songs by Arthur Prysock, Sarah Vaughn and Frank Sinatra, but he loved Dinah Washington the most. Ours was a house of music, fun and dance.

I clearly recall being at home listening to Ray Charles on the radio singing, "Hit the Road Jack," when Mom came into the room and told me that Grandma Louise had died. She was still a young woman and had suffered from a brain aneurysm, while working as a cook for a doctor and his wife on the Upper West Side of Manhattan. She passed out in their home, and the doctor's wife called the paramedics. They came and took her to the nearest hospital, but Grandma went into a coma and never regained consciousness. She passed away a few days later.

My grandmother had not been sick prior to her death, so it came as a shock to everyone because it was so unexpected. It especially shocked Mom. I also felt deeply hurt, and can remember asking God why He let my grandma die. It had only been two years before that she took me down the street to my first dance class. Even though I inherited my talent from Grandma Beatrice, it was Grandma Louise who recognized that talent in me and enrolled me in my first dance class. She told Mom to keep me in dance and Mom, as always, did as my grandmother wished.

Her death changed our lives. I felt that I had grown up a bit and yet I was still a child, a child who had to be told

that all people die and, although they do, God is still a loving
and wonderful God. It is difficult for children to understand
death, but eventually they do. Grandma and I were very close
before she passed away. I believe a spiritual bond had been
formed between Grandma, Mom and I from that time on, a
bond of love that is in our spirits now and forever.

One day while Mom and I sat talking, I noticed something indescribable in her eyes. I didn't quite understand why
then, but deeply thought that when Mom looks into my eyes
I cannot lie to her. I will never forget that strange feeling.
Even as a child I saw that there was a truth and purity in her
soul. That's when I made up mind to help Mom by working
with her in all that she tried to do with her children in life. I
felt she needed a friend, someone who could understand her
quiet, silent and deep spirit.

Mom was alone dealing with her mother's death. Although Dad was there to help her through, she had no brothers or sisters to comfort her and share in the grieving process,
as siblings do together when they lose a parent. Being the
oldest of five children, I understood how just knowing you
had siblings could be such a comfort and support at times like
this. I wanted to take care of Mom even then as a child.

I did the best I could, trying to behave as she wished and
not give her any grief. I became Mom's little helper—that's
what she called me—assisting her in any way possible. As her
little helper, I did all I could to aid in taking care of my siblings. I was like their sister-mom.

Despite my commitment to help Mom, she had to hire
a babysitter to take care of us when we came home from
school. She was working as a bookkeeper for a company

called National Flag on 34th Street in Manhattan, and didn't get home to well after school ended for the day. Finding a good babysitter, even back then, was very difficult. I remember one of the ladies she hired, wouldn't feed us the food Mom left for us to eat after getting home from school. She always waited until it was time for Mom to come home and then feed us. This became a major problem when my baby brother passed out because he hadn't eaten all day. I was standing there when it happened. My brother's food was sitting on the table in the paper bag that Mom left for him that morning. I told Mom what happened when she got home. From then on it became my responsibility to make sure that my baby brother would eat as soon as I got home from school.

The summer I turned nine years old, I volunteered to take care of the boys. She agreed but guided and checked on me during the day. My baby sisters were under the care of Miss Carnell, Mom's closest friend and our next door neighbor. My sisters were very young and Mom trusted her friend because she was an older lady who loved kids but never had any of her own. Well to tell the truth, she particularly liked taking care of little girls. She always said boys were too hard for her to handle, plus she loved dressing little girls in pretty clothes and doing their hair with fancy bows. I must admit she took very good care of my sisters.

I was excited helping Mom with the boys because I knew I would be a better babysitter than the ones Mom had hired, and they all failed. I stepped in for Mom and now she didn't have to worry about how her children were being treated while she was at work. Miss Carnell had the girls and I had the boys.

It never occurred to me then that Mom might be very nervous about her three little kids being at home alone for the summer. If she was nervous, she never let me know. She always showed confidence in me and encouraged me. Also, if there was an emergency or anything, we could run next door to Miss Carnell's. Mom said I was a great babysitter, and with her faith in me, I was eager to show her that I was the best babysitter ever.

By the time Mom got to work at 9:00 a.m. I had already fed my brothers their breakfast, then I would call her to let her know we had all eaten. After that, I'd wash their faces, brush their hair, and they would brush their teeth. Then, I would iron their clothes for the day. We would go outside and play from 10 a.m. until noon. I would take them back upstairs and feed them lunch, and Mom would always call at about 12:10 p.m. to make sure we were upstairs and safe. We had to stay inside and watch television until 3:00 p.m., and Mom again called and we would go back downstairs to play in the park until we saw her coming from the train station at about 5:30 p.m.

Mom always said that it was a good thing that she worked for a small business, because she could always answer the phone when we called. She also said I did better than any other babysitter. It's different these days. There would be a problem if you left children at home alone at that age.

The following few summers, my siblings and I went to a summer program designed to help expose inner-city children to arts and crafts. We had classes from 9:00 a.m. until 5:00 p.m., just like being on a job. The program was designed to teach us music, dance, photography and many other forms of art. I chose dance, of course. I made my brothers take dance with me, that way I could keep an eye on them. The girls were still being watched by Mss. Carnell, so it all worked out perfectly. We danced and learned many new methods, such as the Katherine Dunham techniques taught to us by many beautifully trained dancers.

The program was perfect for inner-city children; everyone in the neighborhood learned a new art. At the end of the summer, one of the dance teachers, Nina Garland, took my brothers to an audition for the Metropolitan Opera. They needed two little black boys to dance and sing in a few of the scenes in the opera, Aida. They both were cast in the show. This was all extremely exciting for our family. We were so proud of them because the Metropolitan Opera House was one of the best in the world, and our boys were performing there. That's right, I did say our boys. I felt like they were my children more than they were my brothers, because I always wanted to take care of them. Whenever Mom, Dad and I talked about the boys we would always say our boys; Mom's, Dad's and mine.

The boys performed in Aida a few nights every week for four years. Although they performed two nights a week, they still had plenty of time to learn how to sing. Since I still watched over my brothers in the summer, I formed a group with them called The Young Temps. Mom had no idea how talented we were, so one evening just before she got home we decided to surprise her.

"Come on let's perform for Mom when she walks through the door," I said. I picked out the song called, "My Cloud," by Joe Bataan. It was the first song they sang and Kyle would sing it so well, people would stop to listen when we were performing outside in front of our apartment.

The Young Temps was a wonderful group. My brother Kyle sang lead and my other brother Trell, my sister Debbie and their friend Cedric sang back up and danced. I choreographed all the moves. I was the dancer in the family, and I loved to make up all the steps for the group. I choreographed moves to all the latest songs. I'd sit in my living room and play a record, and mental pictures would just come to me. Stories fitting the songs would also come to me. I didn't realize it then, but I was creating videos for the songs. I'd do the movements according to the words and move according to the melody. It was like I was dancing the dream of the singer. That's how it felt to me. We didn't have VCR's or MTV. It all came from memory and creativity.

I had a number of innovative ideas back then, long before they would ever become my creation. Since I loved music and dancing, and creating scenes from the music, I really did not like it when I was creating a scene in my head and Mom would interrupt me and ask me to run to the store. I would lose my thought or creative mood because I had to turn off the record player until I got back. That's when I wished I had what we have today; music playing in your ears while you're walking down the street. Not a loud boom box, but music that's only in your ear; music just for you. I thought about how cool it would have been to hear music while going to the store for Mom. Now we have music for all of our gadgets.

My two brothers were and still are today two of the greatest singers I have ever heard. I loved to hear them sing and so did Mom and Dad. Their voices complemented each other so well. They sang everywhere around town, and managed to win four weeks singing at the famous Apollo Theater in Harlem. They shared the stage with many of the big, well-known groups back then, groups like The Manhattans, The Delphonics, The Unifics, and The Five Stairsteps.

We all had a lot fun, they as the singers and me as the manager. Well, really I was still just a kid myself, so really Mom and Dad did the managing. But I actually did the choreography. I loved choreographing back then and still do today. Working with my singing group, The Young Temps, made my family so proud. Dad took the group around town to their shows most of the time, but I would be right there, too, watching over them like a second mother hen when Mom wasn't there.

Mom lined up the shows for us. We performed all over Brooklyn and Manhattan, and the name Young Temps became famous around town. Mom remained the one behind the scenes making it all happen. She was an amazing manager, because she had the insight and foresight that it took to navigate through the tough entertainment world in New York.

Mom's sweet, beautiful voice could open any door, and it did. If someone said, "no" to her and it was something she felt had to be done, that "no" only meant there was another way to accomplish her goal. Believe me, she would find that other way, too. Mom told me her mother once said to her, "Eula, once you get something in your head to do, nothing will stop you." My grandmother was right about that.

I can remember when Pearl Bailey was performing on Broadway in the musical, *Hello Dolly*. Mom took us to see the show and when we got home, she told me that she would try to get Miss Bailey to see The Young Temps. Mom called the telephone operator and asked for Pearl Bailey's phone number. The operator responded that she had an unlisted number and a listed one.

"Could you please give them both to me," Mom asked in her sweetest voice.

The operator not only gave Mom the listed number but her unlisted number as well. She never understood why the operator gave her both numbers but was happy she did. Mom called the listed number but no one answered. Then she tried the unlisted one and to her surprise, Miss Bailey answered the phone.

"Ms. Bailey, my name is Eula Stanislaus and I would…"

"How did you get this number," Ms. Bailey interrupted Mom.

"This is my home number," Ms. Bailey scowled. "You are not supposed to have this number."

"I'm sorry, I won't call again," Mom said apologetically and prepared to hang up.

"Well, what do you want?"

"I have two sons, a daughter and one of their friends. They are young and talented and would like them to audition for you." Mom said.

"Do they sing professionally?"

"Yes, around New York mostly."

"Well send their information to my office and I'll take a look at it. Just send it to me." Ms. Bailey gave Mom the address then slammed down the phone.

"Wow, I got through to Pearl Bailey," Mom said to me. "I was just talking to Pearl Bailey. The operator actually gave me her home number."

I listened intently to Mom, but not surprised at all that she had gotten through. She had that kind of persuasive power.

"But she was really upset that I got her home number," Mom continued. "She just said send her some information on the Young Temps and then hung up after I got the address."

To this day I don't know if Mom ever really sent the

information to her. But knowing Mom she probably thought about it and then decided not to do it after all. I think Ms. Bailey's attitude was a disappointment and a big turn off. Mom never spoke a word about the phone call or Ms. Bailey ever again.

The Young Temps were so good that a record company offered them a contract. But about that same time, we got the news that another young singing group of boys had just signed a contract with the famous Motown record label. That group was none other than the Jackson Five. Since the Young Temps, style closely resembled the new young group with Motown, the record company considering our group decided it wouldn't work having two groups out there at the same time that were so much alike.

"If only we had signed you all a couple months earlier, there would have been no problem at all," the executives from the company told us.

We were greatly disappointed but my brothers continued singing and performing in different venues around New York. Eventually my brother Trell landed a part in a Broadway musical, Raisin, which was an adaptation of Lorraine Hansberry's *A Raisin in the Sun*. Trell appeared in that show on Broadway for many years of its run. He had actually replaced Ralph Carter in Raisin. Ralph was going to star in *Good Times* as Michael Evans, my little brother, while my real brother took his place on Broadway. I always thought that was an amazing coincidence.

There was an electricity in the air back then in the late 60's and early 70's, and folks were excited about the changes taking place in the Black community. Black people were on the move, doing and making things happen for themselves. It was a time before PCP and crack cocaine, poisons that I call the "dragon drugs," infiltrated our communities, killing us and tearing us from our dreams and our ambitions. It was a time for hope for all people, but truly a golden time for Black Americans who wanted to be pioneers.

The country had suffered a devastating blow from the assassination of a great man, Dr. Martin Luther King Jr. Because of his death, serious doors that had once been closed to Black people began to open. Dr. King's death was the straw that broke the camel's back. Black America had enough of not being allowed to progress in this country, due to the pure ignorance and superiority the majority of people felt. This brought on the revolution for change.

King's death turned the world around for Black people. Laws were put in place creating job opportunities for minorities, especially Blacks. It was through Dr. King's death that we as Black people could feel a "New Day" in America. In his last speech he said, "I might not get there with you. But I want you to know tonight, that we as a people, will get to the promise land. Mine eyes have seen the glory of the coming of the Lord."

There is a great deal more to this speech, but these few profound lines in this wonderful message meant a lot to me. It showed just how much he realized that his role here on earth mattered. We know that no one wants to die, and certainly not an early age of 39, but when Dr. King spoke that night, he spoke with God's grace all over him. He spoke as if he knew his destiny. We were so proud of Dr. King back then, as we are now. But we as a people must never forget what he sacrificed for us, and how he helped move us forward.

The 1960's and 70's were a time when Afros and dashikis were worn with great pride. Hot pants, bell bottoms and big floppy hats could be seen everywhere. It really was a time when we, as a people, embraced each other and our culture the most. The streets were echoing the soul sounds of James Brown's "Say it loud. I'm Black and I'm proud." We said it loud! We were Black and we were proud, proud to be moving forward.

Growing up during these times with parents like mine was really fun. All our friends in the neighborhood would always come to our apartment. From early in the morning until late at night, our house was filled with our friends. They all loved my parents because they were both watchful of us and of any children around them, and they were like a set of second parents to our friends.

During these years, everyone seemed to have fun together, playing music and making noise, and if we got bored, we would throw a party. We got hot dogs, buns, potato chips, pretzels, candy and Hi-C, and then we called all our friends and invited them over. During the summer months when we were not in school, we'd have a party any day of the week. When we were in school, we had our parties on a Saturday from 5:00 p.m. to 9:00 p.m. All our friends would be there. We had a packed house! We played the latest records—45's back then—and we danced and had a ball, just like Mom and Dad did at my grandmother's house when they were younger. Growing up in Brownsville was very similar to the life on my TV show *Good Times*.

Living in Brownsville also made you strong. Let's just say you couldn't be a pushover in my neighborhood. Mom and Dad were both very strong, despite being opposite in some ways. But they were similar in the manner they wanted to raise their children. Maybe that's why they worked so well together as parents. They were the best, and did their best. As children we felt loved and secure. Mom and Dad were there for us every day of our lives. That created a great sense of stability for all five children. I'm so grateful for that stability, and those happy times will remain with me forever. It was a great time in life and history to be from the "hood."

3.

WITH FAITH MY MOTHER SPOKE INTO MY LIFE

I was about ten years old and in the fifth grade when my mother spoke prophetic words into my life. There were two girls in my class that I wanted to be my friends ever since the first or second grade. I wanted to be a part of their little clique and I couldn't figure out why they didn't want to play with me. I asked Mom time and time again, "Why don't they want to be my friend?"

"I don't know why," she said.

The question stayed with me for three years. Then, one day I figured it all out. The simple answer was they got all A's and I got B's. I figured if I started getting A's, I'd be accepted into their group. Well, I studied with a great deal of vigor and determination. Finally, we took a major test and all my hard work paid off. I got an A right along with the both of them. They were all surprised as I was also. I thought, now I have arrived and I am in the 'A Lister's Club!'

That day at recess, I went over and asked if I could play double-dutch with them. They looked at me the same way they had in the past.

"No, you can't," they said and continued to jump rope.

Their rejection devastated me because I couldn't understand why I still wasn't accepted by them. I had gotten an A.

I went home hurt and feeling like something must be wrong with me. I kept asking myself why they refused to be my friends. I ran into the house crying.

"Why are you crying, Bern?" Mom asked.

"Because those two girls still don't want to be my friend even though I got an A on my test, just like them," I said.

"It doesn't matter if they don't want to be your friend," Mom said. "They may get A's all the time, but maybe they don't have the talent that you have. You can dance, you can draw, and you can act. Everybody has different talents, but you have something very special, Bern."

"I don't understand," I said to her.

"Don't you know when you come into a room you just light it up? Now that means you have something special," Mom added with a smile.

I didn't know what she was talking about, and even though she tried to encourage me, it didn't seem to matter much because all I wanted at that time was to be accepted by the girls at school. I moped around all evening, still feeling rejected and hurt.

Looking back as an adult, I can say that I always believed Mom was guided to say and do certain things at the right time in our lives. Mom's faith in God was very strong, and she always prayed for guidance. What she said to me that evening I believe was a message God had given her to deliver to me. She came into the living room and sat down right next to me while I remained in that sad place.

She looked at me and quietly said, "Bern, one day the whole world is going to know your name." She said it with such passion and conviction just as if she knew that her words would surely become a reality.

"Okay Mom," I said. I knew she was really trying to get me out of that mood, so I soon snapped out of it and got back to being myself.

Hearing such reassuring words from Mom made an impact on me, that would never leave me. The way in which she spoke them made me believe her. I knew she really wanted me to feel better and just move on. Mom was teaching me to deal with life's rejections, because we all have to deal with rejection from time to time.

I look back at those words she said with such sureness in spirit, and I now know that she had spoken prophecy into my life. I will always remember how she knew, that the words she spoke to me at ten years old would come true. The world does know my name. I used to joke with her and say, "But you didn't tell me they would know me as Thelma before they knew me as Bernadette." We would just laugh and acknowledge that my mother had been right.

I had a mother who spoked positively into my life. She taught me by example, that we as parents must speak into the lives of our children that which we want for them. Empower them with the confidence you have in them, and children listen to your parents!

My desire to be one of those girls eventually just went away. I accepted it for what it was, and continued with my dance and acting classes. When I was about twelve, I went to a dance school in Jamaica, Queens. Mom had searched for a really good school for me, and after scouring all over Brooklyn could not find one. Finally she came upon the one in Queens. We went up there to observe some of the classes and decided I should study there.

The trip to the school from Brownsville took an hour and

a half by train. It was an excellent school, and most of the students had been attending since they were either two or three years old. They were like a large family. When I first began to attend, to my surprise, they treated me like an outsider. The students came from upper-middle-class families, so I had two strikes against me from the start. I was someone coming in at twelve years old and not two, and I was not from the upper-middle-class. I could feel that judgmental attitudes from the moment I walked into the class. They were unfriendly from the teacher on down.

On one occasion, some of the students threw my street shoes away and I had to go home in the dead of winter wearing my ballet slippers. Up until then, I tolerated their ugliness because Mom reiterated that she had me enrolled in the very best dance school for me. But the shoe incident was more than I could bear. I was through with that bunch. I wanted to give up and quit, because of the arrogance of everyone in the school. I dreaded going there every Saturday but Mom would not let me quit.

"You go there and learn as much as you can, and ignore those people," she said to me.

Now, that was truly easier said than done. But I fought through the prejudice and ugly attitudes, and continued to go to the classes every Saturday morning. Mom's persistence and fortitude to not let anyone turn her away from what she knew was best for me helped to solidify my feelings that I really had a great mother. She did not let any obstacles faze her one bit. I followed her lead and ignored those girls as well. I learned to do what I had to and not let someone's feelings about me or my talent stop me.

Mom constantly showed my siblings and me that she

believed in our ability. She always said. "You have to show them what you can do. How else will they know that you even have talent? Let them see how good you are," she advised us. "Don't be shy because those people are just people like you. That's all they are. No one is better than you and you have as much talent as they have, no matter what they think of you."

Little did I know that Mom was building character within me. She refused to let me quit, no matter how much I begged and expressed how uncomfortable I felt while there at the dance class. I thank her for not allowing me to fall victim to other people's opinions and prejudices.

"Keep focus and get on with the business of learning," she constantly said.

In my case becoming a beautiful dancer just like Mom imagined for me was both our reward. That lesson has carried me a long way in my life thus far. If I didn't have faith in my abilities then, I at least lived on the faith that Mom had in me. I thank God for her faith, strength and wisdom.

Dad also passed on words of wisdom. I can recall him saying, "No one can stop you if you are determined to reach a goal. Having the determination to become what you want to be and the discipline to get you there is what you need in this world."

I certainly wouldn't have been the dancer I turned out to be if it weren't for both my parents, who encouraged me to go on when I wanted to quit. I learned if you want to achieve a goal in life, you must be persistent even when life appears to be at its bleakest.

Mom grew up during the golden age of film, an era that was all about movies and movie stars. Executives at MGM and other studios made their stars really shine. They were very glamorous and actually larger than life. Studios would put the star on a weekly salary and provide them with a beautiful home in a neighborhood where all the other stars lived, places like Beverly Hills, Hollywood Hills and Brentwood. They were given the right cars to drive, and the studios let them borrow beautiful clothes to wear whenever they had to make an appearance. The stars were on contract for years at a time. Stars were stars and they were treated as such. Their personal business was always kept private. Whatever got out to the public was designed by their publicity agents.

Mom told me when she was a girl, she wrote to Lena Horne and Lena Horne wrote her back. Mom was so excited to get the autograph signed by the star. She treasured that autograph for a long time. Later she told me that she'd dreamed of becoming a movie star one day. I guess that was the dream of every young lady in those days.

While growing up I learned a lot about the golden days of Hollywood's movie stars because Mom had lots of books about them. I remember looking at the pictures in those books, especially a book about *Porgy and Bess*, starring Sydney Portier, who was Mom's favorite actor. I also enjoyed looking at pictures of Dorothy Dandridge. I watched her movies and admired her work. She was multi-talented. She could sing, dance and act. She was an inspiration to me.

While growing up, Dad always said that I reminded him of her. "If they ever do her life story, you should play her. You and she have the same complexion and the overall same look," Dad told me before I ever became an actress.

It made me feel wonderful knowing that my Dad saw movie star potential in me. I guess on some level, I kept that thought in the back of my mind, and along with the encouragement of my mother, it shaped the path that I took next.

Every Friday night, Mom and I had movie night. I guess you would call it mother and daughter night. I really looked forward to this time with Mom because I had all of her attention. I didn't have to share her with my other siblings. My mom had one on one time with all of her children, but Friday night movies was my time.

I really don't know how Mom ever enjoyed a movie with me along because I was the kind of kid that would tap her on the arm every five minutes to ask, "Mom, what's going to happen now?"

I know that had to be very annoying to her. But Mom didn't seem bothered at all. She would just say, "I don't know. Let's watch and see."

Before the movie would begin, we bought hot buttered popcorn and Almond Joys, our two favorites. I mean, how could you really enjoy a movie without hot buttered popcorn and Almond Joys? It all went together for me. That was our thing; the movies, popcorn with butter and Almond Joys. I really looked forward to our movie nights. I guess that is how she felt when she, as a little girl, and her mom would go to the movies together. It became a mother-daughter tradition.

Dad would baby sit my brothers and sisters on Friday nights, while Mom and I bonded. But he and I had our own time together also. My special time with him was going to his music rehearsals. Dad also taught me to dance with him. He and I became dancing partners when I turn ten years old. But what I really loved was going to his band practice. The practice always took place in one of the band member's basement. When they would play Calypso music, which is the music of the West Indies, I could not sit still. I had to get up and dance.

As I grew up, I loved going to the dances that Dad's band would host. They were usually held at the St. George Hotel in Brooklyn. Mom would let my best friend Lillian and I go. We were about eleven and would dance the Calypso for what seemed like all night long, while Dad played in the band. It seemed that we danced until sunrise, but in fact the dance ended at two in the morning.

When I went to parties with my parents, Dad and I always danced together and eventually became great dancing partners. We had our routine down. Anytime we danced together, we knew we were the best on the floor. Up until the last weekend of his life, we would go to a West Indian dance given by one of his friends. Dad used to say I was the best partner he ever had, and to this day no one can dance with me like my dad did. I've been all over the world and I still haven't found a dancing partner that can compete with him.

Inspired by Dad's music, Mom's movies and energized by choreographing for my brother's group, I was ready to take the stage and show the world what I could do. But what I wanted to do most, I couldn't and it frustrated me.

In the early 1970's there was only one pageant open for young Black girls who wanted to be beauty queens. At age thirteen, I wanted to compete in the Miss Black New York Pageant, but it was open for girls eighteen and over. True to Mom's natural instinct to help me achieve my goals, she raised the issue why shouldn't there be a pageant for teens?

Mom went to Hal Jackson, head of the pageant and a disc jockey with WBLS an urban adult contemporary FM station in the city.

"Young girls like my daughter need a pageant they can participate in, something for girls ages thirteen to seventeen," Mom suggested to him.

Hal Jackson took Mom's advice and the next summer there was the Miss Black Teenage New York Pageant. Mom never got the credit for giving Mr. Jackson the idea but that didn't bother her. She didn't do it for the credit, she was just being a supportive mother. She showed me that there was always a way for me to achieve my goals, even if I had to make a way for myself.

The next year I entered the pageant and Mom supported me all the way. She bought the gowns, the bathing suits and everything else I needed to participate. I know it was a struggle for both Mom and Dad to buy all the outfits, required for the contestants to wear. Remember, my parents were not rich. But they made it happen for me. I had everything needed and I looked beautiful.

Every Sunday for the next six weeks that summer, Mom got herself and four children ready and we all went to Manhattan for rehearsal. It took an hour to travel from our home to the studio, and then there were four hours of rehearsal. I put in a lot of work to get ready but the Sunday of the contest, I woke up that morning and said to Mom. "I don't want to go to the pageant."

"What?" Mom looked at me as if I was out of my mind. "Look, you better start getting dressed 'cause we have to leave in about an hour."

I thought maybe she didn't hear me. "I don't want to go to the pageant."

Mom had enough. She gave me that mommy look; you know the one, as if to say, "Don't you try it Bernadette."

I knew better than to argue with her. I started getting dressed but with the biggest attitude. My lips were poked out and I moved as slow as molasses. On the ride to Manhattan I was so mad that she made me go, that I decided I would muster up an asthma attack. Okay, yes, I'll admit it. I knew how to make myself have an attack by breathing deeply until I started to wheeze.

There, I got her now, I thought. "Ma…wheeze, wheeze, wheeze, I'm having …wheeze, wheeze, wheeze, an asthma attack and I can't…wheeze, wheeze, wheeze, do the pageant."

Well, mothers know their children, right? By this time, Mom was just about fed up with me. Back in those days you could buy asthma inhalers over the counter. She looked at me and said.

"You see that drugstore over there at the corner?" She pointed at a drugstore. "Well, we're going over there and get a Primatene Mist. You're going to take it and you'll be fine." She paused for emphasis. "Then you're going to get on that stage and do your thing."

By this time I realized that Mom meant business, and I just better get it together. And I did get my act together and went on the stage, did what I was supposed to do and did it well. It was that Sunday when a manager looking for new talent was in the audience. After the pageant ended, he came over to Mom and said.

"We're doing a new TV show, and we're looking for a young lady to play the daughter in the show. It looks like your daughter would be great." He then pulled out his business card from his pocket. "Here, take my card and bring your daughter to the audition at CBS studios tomorrow."

The next day, Mom and I went to the audition at CBS in

Manhattan. There were at least a hundred other girls there. As I sat waiting for my name to be called, I thought about something Dad had said to us: "What's for you no one can take from you." I felt much calmer after repeating his words to myself.

Mom gave me that same calm but serious attitude she had the day of the pageant. She also said. "Just go in there and do your thing."

I knew what that meant— show them my talent and don't be shy. After repeating my dad's advice followed by what Mom said, I felt ready.

They finally called my name and I strolled, filled with confidence, into the room for the audition. I first saw Jimmie, J. J. Walker standing there with that dumb hat on his head and Norman Lear, the producer of the show, sitting behind a desk. He gave me a script to read.

I looked it over and noticed that it just didn't seem like the language a young girl from the projects would use. In fact, it sounded very much like someone not from the project. I asked Norman Lear if I could just improvise instead of reading the script.

He gave me a strange look. It wasn't a bad one. I guess my request amused him as if to say, "This one is different, and bold enough to ask if she cannot read from the script and do her own thing."

"Go ahead, improvise," he nodded.

I walked over to Jimmie and said, "You promised that you'd wash the dishes and take out the garbage. Do something around here."

"No! I'm not doing dishes and the garbage ain't full yet," Jimmie replied.

I hit him on the arm. "You better do something around here!" Then we really started to argue. We said some finny lines and Norman was cracking up. I think that's when he realized that Jimmie and I were natural as brother and sister.

After the CBS audition, it took them about a month to call me back to ask if I could come out to California for a screen test, so Mom and I went to Los Angeles. Three girls and I were in the running. We tested for a week and that consisted of reading in front of the cameras with Jimmie. We went back and forth with various scenarios. It was fun to me. I didn't realize the importance of the audition at that time. Keep in mind this was my very first audition, ever. Maybe that was a good thing, because I just acted very natural and treated J.J. the same way I would treat my real brothers. It was a perfect fit for me from the time I walked into the studio. I was just being me, that girl from the projects in Brownsville, stepping into the role of that girl on that stage in Hollywood.

Thinking back to the Sunday of the Miss Teen Black New York Pageant, I must tell you why I acted up and didn't want to go. I was afraid. I had a strong fear I would not win. I kept asking myself, "Why am I going? I am not going to win. I never won anything like this before. What made this any different?"

The lesson I learned from that situation in my life was not to let fear stop me from walking into my destiny. If I had let fear prevent me from competing in that pageant on that Sunday, I would never have walked into my role of playing Thelma on the first black family television show, *Good Times*.

With Mom's determination and belief in me I did walk into my destiny. I have always thanked her for her wisdom and insight as my mother. I didn't win Miss Black New York

Teen, but I did win the role as Thelma and became the first Black female teenager ever on television.

I remember the day I found out that I got the role. It was on Saturday afternoon while out with a friend. I came home about three o'clock and Kyle told me he'd answered the call about an hour ago. He said that the person on the line asked if Mom was home because it was CBS calling, and they needed to speak to an adult. Mom got on the phone and they told her that I had gotten the part. Mom became so excited she could hardly wait until I came home. I'll never forget the look on my mother's face when I walked through the door into the apartment.

Mom sat on the couch with her legs crossed when I strolled into the living room and our eyes met. I knew something very different had happened. It was a happy sense of knowing, a sense that maybe they had picked me. Mom smiled and said very calmly.

"You go it. You got the part. They want you to be Thelma."

"I got it Mom? I got it? They picked me?" I shrieked. I couldn't believe what I heard. I repeated it over and over and it took days for it to final settle in that I was now going to Hollywood to play the role of Thelma.

That began a whole new life for my entire family. After getting the role, I was able to help Mom and Dad educate my brothers and sisters and move them out of the projects. I had been on the show for about a year when Mom and Dad moved to the Cobble Hill section of Brooklyn. Three of my siblings went to Performing Arts High School and then came out to California to attend University of Southern California. It was truly a Cinderella story for me, like hitting that one in a million shot, or just like winning the lottery.

I thank God for this blessing, because it was, a blessing from God. But my first blessing was to have a mother like Eula and father like Greg. I have always felt blessed to have them as my parents. I felt blessed even before *Good Times*. Mom never gave up on me and was behind me all the way. That's why I made it to where I am today. I have loved her so deeply all of my life, because she also had a very deep love for me.

I was happy that I was cast as Thelma but I was most happy for my mother. All of her hard work finally paid off. I truly felt that, as the devoted mother, she deserved this victory. To me it was her reward because of her strong faith in God. She cultivated her daughter just as a loving mother would do, never realizing that I would become the first black female teenager ever on television. Realizing now that *Good Times* is a part of television history, I know that she felt blessed and I made her very proud.

I always told Mom that my winning the role of Thelma was not only a win for her, but for my grandmother Louise. At two years of age, my grandmother had told Mom, "This one I love, Eula. This is the one." I don't know why she said that, but she put her blessings on me that day. All my life I have felt a very special bond between Grandmother, Mother and me. It felt as if Grandmother was my angel, and now that Mom is with her in heaven, I feel she is also my angel. I feel surrounded by both their love all the time. It is just amazing to feel the presence of both Grandmother and Mother here with me. Our connection is truly eternal.

The lessons I have learned from both Mom and Dad were lessons that shaped me as an adult. It would be some of these lessons that helped me to form my character.

Above: My father's brother Cassion
(l), sister Edith (m) and my father (r)
Below: My father's mother Beatrice

Above: My father and grandfather
Below: My Dad and his Army buddies
(Dad is on the bottom row on the right.)

Above: My mother's father, Wilbert.
Below: My mother's mother, Louise.

My mother and her mother on Easter Sunday

Above: Mom and Dad when they first started dating
Below: Mom and Dad at their engagement party

Above: Mom's wedding invitation

Above: Mom on her wedding day
Below: My parent's wedding reception card

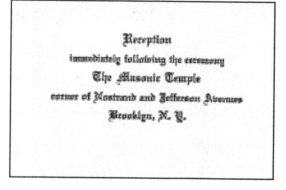

Above: My grandmother Louise and Collis
Below: My grandfather Wilbur and Hattie

4.

YOUNG ADULT YEARS IN HOLLYWOOD

Leaving home and growing into my own in Hollywood was easy in some ways and hard in others. I believe it was more difficult on Mom because she had to go back and forth from New York to California a lot. We had family in California, Uncle George my Grandmother Louise's brother and his family. I lived with them for the first 2 years, and they made my transition easy. My parents were very comfortable with me living with them. That way they knew I'd be well looked after when one of them was not there. Eventually, I got my own apartment in Hollywood. I had a cousin named Sinnora who attended UCLA and lived with me for the first year. The following year she went off to Howard University Medical School. Sinnora became a medical doctor and now practices in Atlanta, Georgia.

My *Good Times* family was very loving and supportive. Looking back on what the show meant to so many people back then and even today, I realize what a powerful impact it really had; the first all-black family show that included a mother and a father. I give a lot of credit to that wonderful actress, Miss Esther Rolle for the show's family structure. Although the producers wanted the show to be a single mother struggling with her three kids, Miss Rolle said,

"No Way. I will not have a show without a father. I grew up with a mother and a father and I want to show America that Black men stay with their wives and their children and raise them just like other races of people do."

That is the reason why *Good Times* had a mother and a father in the home.

Esther told the producers that she knew the perfect actor for the job, and that was John Amos. We all know now that Esther was right. John Amos did such a fine job that children all over the world have told him that he was like their father, especially those who grew up without a one in their home.

Being an author and speaker, I travel and tour all over the United States, and people constantly tell me how much they love *Good Times* and what that show meant to them growing up. Parents tell me that their children watch it, even today. They express to me, with gratitude, the values and lessons it has shared with them. But most of all, they call it safe television. I have been told that they just don't make shows like that anymore.

Twenty-five years ago my dad said that *Good Times* was the first reality television show. Now Dad said that long before reality television existed and he was right. *Good Times* was the real deal. All of our fans want to see the original cast back together doing a movie and another series. I tell them it will happen.

I had a very close and loving relationship with Miss Rolle. She was like my mom in Hollywood. I loved her. I believe that it really made my real mom very relaxed to know that I was close to Esther and she took me under her wings and showed me love like I was her real daughter.

John Amos was a wonderful father figure to us, as well. He was watchful like a father to his kids on the set, very protective of all three of us. He gave me very good advice along the way. He taught me to listen more than speak when dealing with Hollywood brass. It was great advice for someone just beginning in this business. There is a lot to learn when you first start out on a number one television show. Today he is considered one of America's favorite television dads of all times.

Ralph Carter, who played Michael, was like my big, little brother. Ralph is one of the most brilliant men I know. He has been in the entertainment business since childhood. He was a very accomplished Broadway star at the age of ten. His talent and wisdom has afforded him the opportunity to live in many countries in Africa as a young adult.

Jimmie Walker was truly like a big brother to me on and off the set. From the moment he and I met at the audition at CBS, we became like real brother and sister. I always felt very comfortable working with him. He was nice and kind to me, and I thank God I had him to work with; it made being Thelma fun. Jimmie didn't talk much on-set because he was a comic and would go to the comedy clubs at night. So I guess in the mornings when he had to come to the set for rehearsal, he might have been a bit tired. That's why he always remained quiet on the set, but you know me, I would make him talk and he had no choice. I really loved working with both of my television brothers. I genuinely felt like their sister who had to handle two boys.

Ja'Net Dubois played our favorite neighbor, the glamorous Willona. She showed the world that you could have a fun neighbor, who really cared for her friend's family like they were her own. I enjoyed watching her work because she always kept things light and fun. She treated me like she was my aunt and I loved her sense of fashion. I thought she was very talented not only as an actress, but as a singer and songwriter as well. She wrote and sang the theme song, "Moving on Up," for the show

The Jeffersons. I think she wrote that song in a few hours, then said she was going to let Norman Lear, the producer, hear it on our lunch hour. When lunch was over, she came to me and said Norman loved the song and wanted her to also sing it for the opening of the new show.

Johnnie Brown played the janitor Mr. Brookman or as we often called him, Buffalo Butt. He always made us laugh and kept our spirits up. Later in the show, Janet Jackson played Penny. She was the sweetest and perfect little lady. We were so excited to have her on the show.

I remember a very funny story that happened while we taped an episode with Gary Coleman, who eventually went on to star in his own show, Different Strokes. Gary's first television appearance was on *Good Times*, and when he first saw Miss Janet Jackson who was about ten years old at that point, eight-year- old Gary fell in love. He would chase Janet around the set and she would run from him like crazy. Well we were taping the show on Thursday, that was our tape night, I stood behind the stage getting ready to go on and here comes little Janet running as fast as she could toward me.

She grabbed onto me and said, "Bern, can you please tell him to leave me alone?"

I guess Gary felt that if he didn't catch her at this point, he would never have the chance again since after taping the show, his part would be finished.

I went over to little Gary and grabbed him by his arm and said, "Look, stop chasing her. Leave her alone and I mean it! Just stop!"

I believe the tone of my voice scared him. He gave me that half grin, but he left her alone. To this day I am still close to Janet and her family.

I can't forget Ben Powers who played my husband. I was truly hurt upon hearing of his death. On *Good Times* we had a nice and easy working relationship. He was always so professional and exceptionally talented. When they told me that Thelma was getting married on the show, I was excited. They auditioned three finalists to be Keith. I chose Ben Powers and I am glad I did. He was always a good play-husband. He treated me like a queen on the show.

I'm sure you all remember the episode when Keith slapped Thelma because of his drinking problem. Then at the end of the show Thelma had a long talk with him, right? At the end I said "There is one more thing," and I slapped him back. Well, I slapped him so hard I couldn't believe it myself.

When the show ended he came over to me and asked, while holding his face but with a smile, "Did you have to hit me so hard?"

I hugged him and said, "Oh, I'm sorry Ben."

He returned the hug and we both were glad we never had to slap each other ever again.

Although our working chemistry was perfect on the show, I knew very little about his real life. After the show ended we would call each other on holidays and birthdays, but after 1991 I stopped hearing from Ben, and no one could tell me where he was. I always thought we would see each other again but we never did. I will miss his wonderful, kind soul and his amazing talent.

Today we are still very close as a cast. The show is as popular as it was when it first aired. Esther Rolle would be proud to know that about her show. She passed away on November 17, 1998. We all were saddened by her death because we loved Esther and just like a true family, and we all attended Esther's memorial in Los Angeles.

HOLLYWOOD DAYS

Being in Hollywood really made me understand what Dad had preached to us all of our lives, "What's around you does not have to be in you." I've always said, "Hollywood's got nothing on Brownsville." All of the bad things like drugs, drinking and sex were all around Brownsville too. So being in Hollywood was not a shock to me because I had already seen a lot back in Brooklyn. I was very aware of my surroundings and I was not getting involved with that kind of lifestyle in Hollywood.

People have always asked me, "How come you never got caught up by Hollywood and you are the same person you were before? Hollywood never changed you." My answer is always that Hollywood is just another place in the world and I will remain the person I have always been, no matter where I live." I will always thank Mom and Dad for raising me that way.

Now there were some lessons I had to learn about being a professional actress, and Miss Esther Rolle was definitely my teacher. When I first moved to Los Angeles, I didn't drive but my family drove me everywhere. After my cousin Sinnora moved to D. C., Miss Esther Rolle would drive me to work until I got my driver's license. It was convenient because we lived right around the corner from each other.

We had to be on the set every morning at 9:00 a.m. Esther said that she would be in front of my door at 8:30 a.m. sharp, and she was. I always ran a little late, like two or three minutes, sometimes five minutes.

When I started running ten minutes late, Esther said to me, "Bern, if you continue to be late I am going to leave you."

I said, "Oh, Ma!" That's what I called her, Ma. "I know you won't leave me, right?"

She said, "I will if you are not there at 8:30."

Well, I really didn't believe she would leave me because how would I get to work if she did? It's well known that you can't get a cab in California that easily. Anyway, I really didn't think any more about it. The next morning, I tried to get out by 8:30 but it never fails, when you try so hard to be on time, it seems like everything gets in your way. When I looked at the clock and saw that I was three minutes late, I could hear what Esther said to me the day before.

"I will leave you Bern."

I tried to get there on time, and I'd made an improvement. I wasn't ten minutes late, only three. But it might as well have been fifteen minutes because when I got downstairs, Esther had left me. Now I had to find a way to the set on my own. I called a cab and it didn't get there to pick me up until 11:00 a.m. I didn't get to work until 11:30. When I walked into the rehearsal hall, Esther had this look on her face like I told you I would.

That day I understood that I was in the big leagues and there was no time for foolishness. It upset me for a minute but I learned a lesson. As a professional actress on a professional show, I had to become a professional and be on time for work. I'm grateful to Esther every day because thanks to her leaving me that one time, I have always been on time for work since then.

One day while at Esther's house, where I spent most of the time and where we went over our lines I said, "Ma, I'd like to have more lines on the show. We've been filming for over six months, and I feel my character needs to say more than, 'Hi Mom, hi Dad, shut up J.J.,' and then I'm back in the bathroom."

Esther looked at me and asked, "Oh, really? So, you think you can handle more lines?"

"Yes Ma, I really do think I can handle it. In fact, I know I can handle it."

She thought about it for a while then said, "Okay, then, let me take care of it."

I felt relieved because I knew if Esther said she would take care of things, they would get taken care of. She was the star of the show; let's not forget that. When Friday came, the day that we read for the next week's show, I had my usual few lines in the script. At the end of the table read they always asked Esther how she liked the script.

"I have a question to ask," she said. "Are you ashamed of my daughter? Is she retarded or something?"

Her question shocked me and I was hoping the producers would definitely say, "No."

"Why are you asking that Esther?" the producers asked.

"Because my daughter is always in the bathroom and she doesn't have a lot to say. J.J. has a voice. My son, Michael, has a voice. Now I want my daughter to have a voice, also."

"Certainly Esther. We can do that," the producers said.

From that day on my character, Thelma, had a voice on *Good Times.* I have always loved and admired Esther for taking up the banner and fighting for not only me, but so many others who were treated fairly on her show. This included those in makeup, hair and wardrobe. She was an awesome leader for us. I will always be grateful to Miss Esther Rolle, for giving the first black female teenager on television a voice with opinions and differing attitudes, for many young girls to identify with. Thelma represented the young, teenage girls of every race. She always had something going on in her life that any girl could identify with.

Being a dancer and from New York, I kept my New York style even though I now lived in Los Angeles. We dancers always wore leotards with our dance pants when we were out. That was our usual when running around the city to our dance classes. Those clothes were skin tight but easy to get into with no fuss. I always wore tight clothes because they felt comfortable on my body. I also loved to wear high heels. Girls in their early teens in the mid-seventies wore high heels, and they were usually platform shoes. So when not in dance class, where we wore flat dance shoes, we always wore high heels. Well, at least I always did.

There I was in Hollywood, where Thelma had to wear mostly jeans that teens wore then. Well, the wardrobe woman, Mrs. Adella Farmar, who was responsible for our clothes on the show, would go buy our outfits in Century City. They had beautiful clothes of great quality, but none could fit me the way I felt comfortable. Adella and I came up with a solution. She bought me some very nice burgundy platform shoes that gave me my high heel feeling. Then she bought me a few jeans and some blouses that a girl who lived in the projects of Chicago would wear.

"Let's see what we can do with these things to make you feel comfortable," she said.

Mrs. Adella and I worked together on what I liked, which for me meant the jeans in on both the outside and the inside seams all the way down to the knees. I then asked her to take out all the pockets in my jeans, and she would sew them down, forming a smooth surface on all sides. Finally she put darts in front, back and on the sides of my tops, forming a complete flat surface for the blouse to lay on me like a fitted glove. My work clothes were a second skin just like my dance clothes, and I finally felt comfortable. I decided to wear panty hose under the pants making for a smooth silhouette.

Well what do you know? I started a trend with my new and improved wardrobe, and girls all over the country that looked up to me wanted to dress like me. The tight jeans and tight sweaters and blouses became the fashion back then, and we even see women dressing in that style today.

That's how those tight jeans were born to our American audience. Before my character, there were no such fitted clothes in existence. The tight jeans and fitted tops were truly created by me out of the need for my clothes to fit like dance wear, and by Mrs. Adella's knowledge and acceptance of what look would be best on me for the show. No one has ever given the show credit for being the true innovator of this look that is everywhere today. But I must give credit where credit is due. Adella and I are still close today.

I was in my third year of the show when I noticed that my voice sounded very deep and unnatural. My throat began to hurt when I spoke. In the evenings it got worse. It would hurt to even talk and by the time night rolled around, I could hardly say any words at all.

I decided to go see a specialist. The doctor told me that I needed an operation to remove polyps on my vocal cords, if

I wanted to sound normal again. They told me an operation like this could go one of two ways. I could lose my voice forever or I could come out just fine and my voice would return to normal.

I had the operation and they told me that I should not speak for a few months in order for my vocal cords to heal properly. We relayed to the producers of the show what was going on and they suggested that I learn the script as usual, but don't speak until tape night. I asked my doctor if that would be okay and he agreed that would be fine. That's how I stayed on the show while my vocal cords healed. That was a very frightening time for me, because if the doctor had said I couldn't use my voice just one day a week, Thursday tape night, I would have had to leave the show for a while. But it all worked out fine.

Sometimes things happen for reasons we don't know or understand. Right after the operation, I couldn't use my voice. I had to write out everything in order to communicate. There was no such thing as text messaging back then, but it would have served a great purpose for me if we'd had texting and face time. But since we didn't and writing everything down with no spell check either became too much bother for me to keep up with, I just decide to stop trying to communicate at all, and I became very quiet.

During this time of silence, I started writing poetry. I believe it was God's way of directing me toward another avenue in my life. During those four months of healing, the words started to pour out of me. It seemed as if it came from somewhere deep within. I wrote major pieces, and I am putting together a book of one-hundred of my poems to be released very soon.

It was also during this time in my life that I became a serious writer, and it was the starting point that inspired me to pen the kind of poetry that I write today. Who knew back then that I would go on to author my first book of poetry called, *For Men Only*, plus three other books? I for one had no idea that I would write, *Situations 101: Relationships, The Good, The Bad and The Ugly, Situations 101: Finances, The Good, The Bad and The Ugly*, and this book. I will always believe that it was God's hand that sat me down to be quiet enough to hear the voice within. The temporary death of my physical voice gave birth to my voice as a writer.

Later in life when Miss Esther Rolle's health started to decline, I was so grateful to have been there for her. My daughter, Brittany Rose, only two years old at that time, would be with me when I took Esther to her doctor's appointments on Tuesdays. We made this our very special time, and spent the entire day together, just the three of us. After her doctor's appointment, Esther always wanted to go this soul food restaurant.

I'd say to her, "Ma you're not supposed to eat this kind of food."

She replied, "This is what I have a taste for."

That settled the issue. I could see that she was very ill, so if she wanted her soul food once a week, then let her have it. And she really did enjoy that food. We'd have our collard greens, sweet potatoes and mac and cheese. I'd have fried fish and Esther fried chicken wings. We enjoyed eating our soul food and reminiscing about our days on *Good Times*, and all sorts of mother-daughter conversations. She gave me advice about my daughters and assured me that I was a good mother and my daughters were beautiful girls.

She said, "I am proud of you, Bern."

I read my poetry to Esther the same way I read it to my real mom. They both loved my writing. One day I asked Esther, since she worked with Maya Angelou and they were friends, if she thought that Ms. Angelou would like my poetry as well.

"Absolutely! Of course she would," she answered. "Your poetry is very good Bern." Her words made me feel good knowing that she felt that way about my work.

I remember that last Tuesday I saw Esther. I dropped her off at her home after our usual activities. Before she got out of the car, she held my hand, looked deep into my eyes and said to me.

"Thank you Bern."

"Why? Why are you thanking me, Ma?" I asked

"For being the best daughter anyone could have," she said.

"Oh, Ma thank you!" I exhaled. This felt like a real good-bye, but I didn't want to admit it at that time. A strange feeling came over me. "Ma, I'm going to St. Thomas to do a play there, but I'll be back home next Wednesday. Do you have anyone to take you to your doctor's appointment on Tuesday?" I asked.

"I'll ask Adella to take me," she said. Adella Farmar, the wardrobe mistress on *Good Times* was also her best friend.

"Okay Ma, but I'll be back on Wednesday, and Thursday I'll come over and make you a pot of steamed vegetables."

She looked at me and said. "Okay, I love you Bern."

"I love you too, Ma, you know that," I smiled and we hugged.

She looked at Brittany and smiled at her. "Little Brittany, I love you too, and you be a good girl, okay?"

Brittany had found a butterfly and had it in her hand. She said, "Ma Es, I want you to have this butterfly. I caught it for you."

Esther opened her hand and took the butterfly. "Thank you," she said, then looked at me. "She is so pretty, Bern."

We smiled. I watched Ma until she disappeared inside her house. I didn't know that was the last time I would ever see her. I got back home from St. Thomas on the next Wednesday. The next day I was awakened with the news that Esther had died. Oh my God, I was broken hearted! I really loved that lady. I was so glad we had such a beautiful conversation in the car, and I had a chance to tell her for the last time that I loved her.

I often think of her and all the fun times we had together. I was blessed to have her as my Hollywood mom. She will forever be in my heart.

5.

When Life Changed Forever
The Death of My Father

"Why don't you and your family come back to New York for a while?" Dad suggested while we conducted one of our usual coast-to-coast conversations by phone. Since moving to California, he had made the same request many times before. This time seemed different. Dad sounded much more adamant, like he really needed me to be close to him and Mom. Because he put so much more emphasis on the request, I really thought about it for a while and decided it might be a perfect time to do so. My husband and I were married in the early '80s' and had our first daughter Dior Ravel. Our life in Los Angeles was working out well, but I had always wanted to produce a play in New York. So my husband and I decided the timing was perfect for us to give it a go.

We flew into New York on a cool Sunday afternoon in October. It felt really good to see the smiles on Dad and Mom because we were there with them. I hadn't lived back home since I moved to California, but I traveled back and forth to see them two or three times a year. I'd stay for one or two weeks and then head right back to California. They also came out to Los Angeles to visit me and stay for a week or so. But now, living with Mom and Dad was more fun than I had imagined it would be. It gave them a chance to be with their granddaughter more, and this they loved.

It felt like we were roommates hanging out and going places. We had never experienced New York together and that's exactly what we were doing everyday. We had so much fun. I learned to appreciate my parents as some really cool adults, not just as Mom and Dad. We were like friends, the four of us, and I got really used to them as our running buddies.

Besides adjusting to the cold once again, this was a wonderful time for me. I went so many places and did so many things with my parents. I took them to see plays on Broadway and to jazz clubs in Manhattan and Harlem. I especially felt close to Dad when we frequented some jazz spots like the Blue Note. It felt almost like the old days when we'd go to his band rehearsals together. I was no longer a young girl but this father-daughter time was still so special to me. It was still our thing because my father and I both loved jazz. Dad even started playing his saxophone again.

"Come on, Dad, play for us," I'd say, and he would play for hours and I enjoyed every minute of it.

Dad and I also bowled together; in fact, we were on a bowling team. He showed me how to score more strikes, and his advice was solid as usual. I did bowl more strikes.

We went out dancing and just like old times, Dad and I danced together. We also took the bus up to Atlantic City because Mom loved it there. I was never happier living with my parents than at this time.

Dad and I shared a love for boxing, and we would go to see all of the Tyson fights. Dad loved Mike Tyson, maybe because he came from Brownsville as well. He was proud to see any young person make it out of Brownsville to the big time,

Tyson being no exception. Because Dad always helped young kids and encouraged them to be successful, he felt a sense pride when they succeeded.

Looking back, I thank God for giving me this time with my parents. It made them both so happy, and it made me not only happy but also most grateful for that time we had together. We didn't know why then, but we know now that God graced us with this most beautiful and precious time together. It would be a short five months and three weeks before it would all end.

The third week of March, Dad came into the house acting strange. He dropped everything in the middle of the living room floor and then hurried into the bathroom. I saw him holding his head and looking in the mirror, while throwing cold water on his face. He came out of the bathroom and sat at the kitchen table.

"Are you alright?" I asked him.

He nodded his head yes and we all continued sitting around the table just talking and laughing. Then out of the blue Dad jumped back in time. He mentioned to my nephews visiting with us, an incident that happened three years ago.

"Dad, why are you bringing up all that old stuff?" I asked.

"So you think I don't know what I am talking about, huh?" He said to my oldest, twelve year old nephew Jacques, and ignored my question.

Jacques looked puzzled. My other nephew, Little Trell only eleven years old, and Jacques just laughed it off and kept playing with a ball, throwing it to each other. Trell allowed the ball to hit the floor and it bounced a few times.

"Stop bouncing that ball in the house! If you bounce it one more time I'm going to throw it out the window," Dad scowled.

We all thought that he was kidding, so they bounced the ball again. My dad grabbed the ball in the air and threw it out of the window. We looked on startled at his action. No one could believe what he just did.

Something was very different with Dad, but I didn't know what.

"PaPa, we can't believe you did that. What's wrong PaPa? Why would you throw our ball out the window?" Jacques asked.

"I told you I would throw it out if you bounced it again," Dad scowled.

The two boys left and went outside to get their ball.

What an extreme act, to throw the ball out the window because it was bouncing in the house, I thought. I could see that Dad was upset but not telling us why. I wondered had something happened to him? It would be a little while before I got my answer.

On our bowling night, I asked Dad if he planned to go with us to the bowling alley. He said no, so I left it at that, thinking Dad would be okay. Maybe he was just irritable and needed to stay home and rest.

I changed into my bowling outfit, then hurried out of the house and down to the bowling alley. Later that night, when I walked into the house I stared at Dad sleeping on the couch. That seemed rather strange. Why hadn't he gone to bed in his room?

The next morning, when I got up, Dad and Mom stood in the kitchen cooking breakfast. He seemed normal.

"Greg, tell Bern what you watched on television this morning," Mom said.

"I watched this new pastor named Charles Stanley. He

told his congregation and everyone watching on television, 'Pray because the end is near. Pray.'"

Dad both surprised and stunned me with the passion of his recitation of the minister's message. He always prayed and attended church, but getting up early in the morning and watching a pastor on television was something Mom had never seen him do before. His interest in the pastor's message surprised Mom also, and she chose not to bother him that morning.

"He was really into what the preacher was saying," Mom said to me.

You know how sometimes when you're in church, you feel like the pastor is talking directly to you. Well that message was especially for Dad that Sunday because it would be the last sermon he'd ever hear.

Mom and Dad had plans to vacation in the West Indies the next weekend. They had been preparing all week for their trip. Dad wanted to get some sneakers for the trip so he, along with my husband and I, got dressed to go to the mall. We decided to take the bus to King's Plaza in Brooklyn. While on the bus, I noticed Dad staring at me.

"Why is my dad staring at me like that?" I asked my husband.

"Because he loves you, Bern," he said.

I often wonder now if my dad was trying to remember me or if he felt something was going wrong with him? I'll never know what that stare really meant, but I know my husband had it right; Dad loved me very much.

We arrived at the mall and found the store where Dad bought his sneakers. He laughed and joked with the salesman asking, "Are there any discounts for seniors?" He took pride in his senior citizen status. Dad loved the seniors. I believe he felt that if a person had lived long enough to reach sixty-five in this world, he or she had accomplished a great thing. Besides, Dad was a spry, very together senior. He may have been sixty-five years old, but he looked no older than fifty.

Once Mom told me that every time she and Dad went to a party or a dance, he always danced with all of the older ladies there.

"Why did he do that, Mom? Do you know why?" I asked.

"Your dad told me that he danced with the old ladies because they came to the party to have fun and they wanted to dance, too," she explained. "But they had no one to dance with them and the men didn't ask them. That's why he made his rounds and asked them to dance. He wanted them to enjoy themselves, too."

"Wow, that's something that he would do that," I said. To me that was the special, caring and loving nature of dad to do that for the older women who may have never been asked to dance.

After Dad bought his sneakers, he turned to me and said, "Bern, do you want a pair? I'll get them for you."

"No, Dad I'm okay. You just get yours," I said.

On our way out of the mall he wanted to get a soda. He and I stopped and bought ourselves a couple of cold drinks. While sitting and drinking, Dad wanted to know where my husband had gone. He seemed a bit concerned and I reassured him that he would be back in a few minutes. He had gone to look at something in another store. It wasn't like Dad to worry about someone's whereabouts like he did that day. He acted very confused, like he really didn't understand why my husband wasn't with us.

"Don't worry Dad, he'll be back," I assured him.

Not long after, my husband met back up with us and we took the bus home. When we got there, Dad put his sneakers on and Mom said. "So you're going to go show your sneakers off to your friends, huh?"

They laughed. This was the first pair of sneakers my dad ever bought and I think the first time he even worn a pair. Dad was a very sharp dresser. I had never seen him in anything but polished dress shoes.

I watched as he walked out the door, and then from the living room window as he strolled down the street. He had a very cool walk. He walked that walk until he made a left turn around the corner, and I couldn't see him anymore.

"Watching your dad walk in his new sneakers huh, Bern?" Mom asked.

"Yes," I said and we both smiled. I don't know what made me watch him that closely. I didn't know that would be the last time I would see him ever walk again.

About three hours later Dad sauntered back to the house. I knew he was at the door because I heard the keys rattling. But it was odd that he didn't come inside. Mom went to the door and opened it. There Dad stood, as if he was shocked that he could not put the key in the keyhole.

"Eula, I have an incredible pain over my left eye," Dad said. "I don't understand. Eula, I couldn't put the key in the keyhole. I don't understand what's happening."

After getting him inside the apartment Mom said, "Sit down here, Greg." He sat down and Mom looked him over. "Come on and lie down a minute," she instructed.

Dad tried to get up from the chair but couldn't.

Mom then said, "You're going to the hospital, right now."

She ran into the bedroom and called 911. Dad managed to get up from the chair and struggled over to the couch. He sat down and asked me to get him a cold towel.

"Dad, maybe a hot one would be better," I suggested.

"No, a cold one," he insisted.

"Okay, where does it hurt, Dad?" I asked.

He took his left hand and tried to point to the area of his head that hurt him over his left ear. As he attempted to reach and touch his head, he slurred his words. It sounded like a computer unplugged and slowly shutting down. Dad had been sitting on the couch, and when he stopped talking his head dropped to his chest. He didn't fall over or anything, he just sat there. We were so scared.

"Dad went down!" I yelled.

Mom told me that the 911 operator said he might be having a stroke, so I should put him on his side. As I laid Dad down on the couch and on his side, I heard this weird, gurgling sound and very deep breathing for a few seconds. Then, it stopped. I noticed he was no longer breathing. I didn't know that the awful sound Dad made was the death rattle, a sound that is made when life is leaving your body. I had never heard anything like it before.

"He stopped breathing!" I screamed.

Mom came out of the other room and ran to Dad's side.

"Greg, please! You can't leave me like this! You can't die on me like this! You've been with me since I was sixteen years old. What am I going to do without you? Greg, please! Don't leave me! Don't die, Greg! Greg, don't die!"

As someone dies, the body doesn't stop functioning all at once. The hearing is one of the last senses to go. It can take up to fifteen minutes before a person stops hearing completely.

Mom remembered a nurse explaining this to her when her mom died. So in our hearts we know Dad heard Mommy crying and pleading.

Suddenly, Dad took a breath and opened his eyes. It was a miracle! He was always a strong, determined man, but to come back from the brink of death had to be a hard thing to do. Yes, my dad started to breathe! Believe me, Dad did this for Mom. He came back and we were elated!

The paramedics knocked at the door, came in and then took Dad in the ambulance. I couldn't believe this was happening to my father. I asked God, "Is this the end?"

I felt a deep, wrenching pain in my stomach and in my heart. When we got to Caledonia Hospital, the nightmare had just started. They brought Dad into Emergency, and a male nurse on staff paid no attention to him whatsoever. My dad laid there going through convulsions and seizures right in front of their eyes, and that male nurse did absolutely nothing.

"Please, do something! Can't you see he's going into convulsions?" we pleaded. The nurse moved at a snail's pace and never went over to help Daddy. We sat there for about ten to fifteen minutes while my father's body shook and convulsed.

We decided to get Dad out of there and take him to Brooklyn Hospital. We called the ambulance to come get him, and just before my brothers started to pick him up and carry him out of there, the ambulance came. Thank God, Caledonia Hospital is no longer there. I am sure from what we saw, more people died in there than were saved.

When Dad got to Brooklyn Hospital, they immediately started working on him. The doctors said that once they got him stabilized they would be able to let us know exactly what was going on. But they could tell us now that his blood pressure was dropping fast and they couldn't operate on him until it went back up. During this time that he was in the emergency room, they were frantically working to keep him alive.

My mother was in shock. We all were. We had no idea what was going on with Dad. They had been working on him for about three hours. The nurse finally came into the waiting room where my four siblings, my mom, my husband and I were waiting. We were all on edge, anxious for an update on Dad's condition.

She told us, "His pressure is not going up, and at this point we don't know if he is going to make it through the night."

It was about two in the morning. The nurse asked us to go back and say our last goodbyes to my father. This didn't feel real. It was like a nightmare that happened all of a sudden. We were not prepared for this.

We all went into Dad's room. I looked over at my mother standing in the doorway. Dad was not in his usual place next to her. I felt unnerved at that moment. Maybe it was God letting me know that Dad would never stand with her again.

I went over to Mom and asked if she felt okay. She nodded yes, but I know she didn't. This turn of events had to be so painful for her.

I walked over to Dad's bed, and kissed him on his cheek. "Dad, I love you so much. Dad, don't die," I pleaded.

Mom went over to Dad and kissed him on the forehead. She leaned over and hugged him and said something in his ear. Then, she turned to leave. As we were walking out, he just looked so sad lying there. I couldn't believe this was it for Dad. How could it be?

We returned to the waiting room, and the nurse said, "If there is even a slight chance, that his pressure goes up a bit, we will call for the neurosurgeon to come in." That was at least something for us to hold onto.

Our family continued praying, asking God to bring his pressure up so that he could have the brain operation the doctors said he needed. An hour had passed, and the nurse came back saying his pressure did go up and that they had called for the surgeon to come in. That sounded like a miracle to us, and we thanked God!

The neurosurgeon, a young African doctor, walked into the waiting room about half an hour later. He looked directly at Mom. "I can't operate yet, but if there is a window for me to do so, I will. Even if there is the slightest window what so ever, I will go in," he said with emphasis. "But, I must be honest with you. Your husband is sixty-six years old and if we operate his chances of survival are slim."

"Okay, but please do your best," Mom whispered.

"As soon as I am comfortable about your husband's chances of surviving the operation, I'll let you know." He finished, turned and left the room.

Unable to sit still, I paced the room waiting for the doctor to return. Another hour or so passed, and finally the door swung open and the doctor stood there looking at Mom.

"I believe we have the window of opportunity we were waiting for in order to operate. We will be operating in the next half hour," he announced.

We all breathed a deep sigh of relief as the doctor turned and walked out of the room. Now the waiting would begin. We knew the operation would take hours but none of my siblings, husband and a few friends even considered leaving Mom before it was over. Somehow we managed to doze off and on.

Early in the morning, the doctor finally came back into the room and we all immediately sat up anticipating his every word. "He made it through," he said. "He's been taken to ICU for close monitoring. He still has a long ways to go but he is now recovering."

His words gave us hope and we felt optimistic about Dad's chances. But what he told us next, tempered our enthusiasm.

"It was a very difficult operation," he began. "The pressure in his head was so strong that the moment we opened him up, blood shot straight to the ceiling. But we made it through." He paused for a second to let his words resonate with us. "But when you go into visit with him, be prepared for what you'll see," he added.

When we finally went into the ICU to see Dad after the operation, we could see how swollen his head was, and it alarmed me. But he was still alive and we could talk to him and hold his hand. I was thankful for that. He was so strong to have come through all of that pain. I can't imagine how hard and awful it was for him to endure it all, for the sake of Mom and his kids. I know Dad held on so that we would have more time with him.

After about two weeks, Dad came down from ICU into a regular room. The swelling had gone down, and there was a small bandage on his head. I noticed four deep impressions on the left side of his head, right over his left ear near his temple. I was in disbelief, and at that point realized what had really happened to him. Based on the imprint on the side of his head, it looked like my dad had been hit with brass knuckles. The blows had been so intense that they left the four prints in his skull. They were branded marks that everyone could easily see on his shaved head.

"Someone did this to my father. They put him here," I pointed to the marks on Dad.

We filed police reports, and if my father died, this would be considered a murder. The police immediately began an investigation. We learned that my father was indeed hit with brass knuckles, by four boys from another neighborhood. Everyone knew my dad in his neighborhood but those boys were from somewhere else and they didn't know him. To them, he was just an older man with white hair.

The police later told us that a witness did see the attack on my father, and that he'd fought with his assailants. But he'd already been struck and there wasn't much he could do. He never saw them coming because they snuck up behind him. After the attack, Dad still managed to pick up his bags and make it home.

Being hit over his left ear, near his temple, caused the blood in his brain to start erasing his memory. That's why he couldn't tell us what had happened to him that Saturday afternoon. I now understood why he had been so impatient with my nephews. Looking back, maybe the sound of the bouncing ball hurt his head or may have been exceptionally loud to him.

Mom had told me that when she had gone to the store the evening that he was attacked, she had seen Dad across the street on his way home. When she saw him she thought, I have never seen Greg walk like that with his head down. He was walking like an old man. It wasn't the spry pep in his step walk, like he always had.

Now we knew why. The attack must have just happened when Mom saw him from across the street.

"No one had to do that to him," Mom said. "Greg was

always helping people in any way he could. Why would they do that to him? They didn't have to hit him with anything. He was a small man."

Dad remained in a coma for about two weeks when the doctor told us his eyes would open automatically after twenty-one days. True to the doctors words, on the twenty-first day Dad's eyes did open, but he was still in a coma.

It appeared that Dad's condition had improved. We felt that he could hear us because he would move his right hand from time to time. We did notice that he never moved his left hand. It remained paralyzed, and after a few weeks we also noticed that his hands and feet were getting cold.

Dad stayed in that state, only getting slightly better. He held on for seven weeks, enough time for us to get used to the idea that he may not be with us much longer. I still thank God for giving us that time so we could adjust.

I remember my last night with Dad so vividly because it had been such an unusual day. Daddy managed to move his arm that had been paralyzed from the hit. He stayed focused the whole day while we communicated with him. We sincerely believed that he was back to being Daddy, and knew in our hearts that he would pull through. He seemed aware of everything, answering us if we asked him a question by squeezing our hand.

Dad had been up from the very early hours of the morning, and by the end of the day we could see he was very tired. He had been up at this point for more than 12 hours straight. He would close his eyes and force them back open, like a person who fought sleep.

We all stayed at the hospital until late that night. It was about nine o'clock when Mom made a very cogent observation. She said, "It's just the seven of us here. Me, Dad and all five of our children."

We then all surrounded Daddy's bed. We held hands and said our prayers. It had been a blessed day and we were so grateful Daddy was recovering. Daddy looked at each and every one of us, staring at us for a very long time, as if he prepared to take the memory of each one of us with him. We were so happy because we knew Daddy had really communicated with each of us. We could read in his eyes that he was saying, "I love you."

After all of my brothers and sisters had gone home, Mom and I stayed in the room with Daddy. Mom could see how tired he was, straining to keep his eyes open. She went over to the bed and said.

"It's okay Greg. You can close your eyes and get some sleep. Get some rest now. I'm here. I'll be sitting over there. I'm here all night with you. When you wake up, I'll still be sitting here."

Dad still didn't close his eyes, I guess because I was still there, and he continued looking at us. Mom turned to me and said.

"Berne. I'm just fine so go home and get some rest. I'll let you all know if there is a change in your dad's condition."

I left but told Dad and Mom that I would be back early in the morning. Mom never left him alone at night; she stayed right there with him from the first night until the last night.

The next morning I went up to Dad's room just as Mom came out. I could tell by her expression that something was wrong.

"What happened?" I asked her.

She looked at me and said, "We lost him, but they're trying to bring his pulse back. They brought it back once, but it faded and they couldn't bring it back again."

Just then, the doctor came out and said, "He is gone."

"He's dead? Greg is gone? He's gone?" Mom asked.

"They killed him! Those damn boys killed him! They killed my daddy!" I screamed.

That night we spent at Kyle's home. The next morning we got together in his living room. Mom came into the room and exclaimed.

"Well, that part of my life is over. I'm done now."

"Mom you are still young, too young to be done," Kyle said.

"No, that's it for me. I have had the best," she uttered.

Mom must have felt extremely lonely after losing my father. She was only fifty-nine when Dad died. I remember Dad used to ask Mom, "Eula, what would you do if something happened to me?"

"Oh Greg, nothing is going to happen to you," she'd always reply.

Dad knew Mom very well; she was devoted to her family and to him. He knew that she had never had to deal with the world alone. The day Dad died I looked at my mom and felt so sorry for her. We all knew what she meant: she planned to remain single. And that's exactly what she did. She stayed devoted to my father forever. She never even entertained the thought of another man. Mom was a very special person.

Dad once said to me, "There is no other woman like your mother. She is the best they got."

I knew what he meant and he definitely had it right, she really was a special person.

The day of the funeral, we dressed in all white to celebrate Dad's beautiful life. The family laid him to rest in white silk pajamas and a gold and white African hat that was made for him by my sister-in-law, Ruth. Dad's skin was a beautiful, olive color against the white silk fabric. He looked like a royal prince.

Friends came from all over to show their respect. The family and friends who came to the church packed the cathedral causing crowds to gather outside, waiting to see him. Dad had so many friends, both old and young.

During Dad's service, my two brothers strolled up to the pulpit and Kyle said.

"Dad we are going to sing your song for you for the last time and we will never sing it again after this."

They sang "On the Wings of Love" by Jeffery Osborne. There wasn't a dry eye in the whole room, including Kyle and Trell. It was a beautiful but painful moment for my brothers, but I am sure they made Dad proud of them once again.

We laid Dad to rest in the Veteran's Cemetery. They buried him twelve feet underground rather than six. He'd always said that he and Mom would be in the same plot together, and when Mom's day came her casket would be placed right on top of his, joining them together again.

I learned a lot about my Dad that day. The stories that so many told about him that afternoon fascinated me, because they were stories of the good deeds he did for others that he never told anyone about. Dad helped so many and taught them valuable lessons about life. He was such a learned and loved man. He once told me that he could talk on any subject with anyone except with a medical doctor. But that was only because he had never studied medicine.

Dad really was the people's star. Everyone who met him loved him. A few years ago I ran into Al Sharpton, who came from Brownsville as well, and he asked me about my dad.

"He passed away," I informed him.

After offering his condolences, he shared a story about Dad with me.

"Mr. Stanislaus was a true activist," he began. "Your father would gather me and some of the young men in the neighborhood, you know, twelve or thirteen-year-old boys, and talk to us. Your father would encourage us to organize. He would say, 'you are young men with a lot of energy. Use it for the positive. Take your energy and put it in the right direction.' Then he would ask us what we wanted to see change in the community, and he would teach us to organize our thoughts. He would tell us to go to our congressmen to present our views. Mr. Stanislaus taught us how to make an effective change, instead of complaining about what we didn't like to each other."

My heart filled with pride and joy as I listened. I'd heard many stories about my father, but hearing this one coming from Al Sharpton, meant a lot to me.

"Mr. Stanislaus was the first man I ever saw with swagger," Sharpton said with a hearty laugh. "Mr. Stanislaus had swagger before Obama."

Reverend Sharpton perfectly described Dad. He was a sharp, cool dude and he truly had that swag. I realized that Dad did a lot to help a lot of people, and he never talked about it. He was fearless and I'll always be proud to call him Dad.

On May 29, 1991, they ruled Dad's death a homicide. They caught the four boys, who killed him, and they are in jail, but that offers only a little comfort. Nothing can take away the pain of my dad being taken from us too soon.

It took our family years to get over the shock of someone in our family being murdered. We found out that my father's attackers had hit four other older men the same way they hit him. Two of the men lived and two of them died. But thank God these four murderers will never hurt another soul. They have been put away forever.

Rest in peace, Dad, your work is done.

THE YOUNG TEMPS

Gregory   Talbert   Cedrik   Debbie

Above: The Young Temps
Below: Me in dance class.

Above: A picture on the set of *Good Times*
Below: My audition photo for *Good Times*

Above left and right: Acting in my first play
Below: Acting headshot

Above: An acting headshot
Below: My daughter Dior, my twin.

6.

MOM'S LIFE AFTER DAD'S DEATH

Life changed for Mom after Dad passed away. I could see that she struggled to pull it together, because this was quite an adjustment for her. My siblings and I thought it best that Mom move closer to one of her children. My baby sister, Yolanda, was in her last year at Hofstra University, and my sister Debbie and my brother Kyle lived in New Jersey. My husband and I had gone back to our home in California, and we were busy raising our oldest daughter, Dior. Mom downsized into a two-bedroom condo close to my brother Trell, but still in the same neighborhood in Cobble Hill. It helped her being close to Trell and his two children, Little Trell and Sharrell.

Mom continued working at this point. She never had a big social life; but enjoyed playing bingo at the church and, of course, going to the movies. She kept busy with all of her children and grandchildren. Mom appeared to be making a successful adjustment in her life.

We talked every day, as usual. I had asked her to come out to California to live with me several times but she always said, "I have to help Trell with the kids." That wasn't the only reason for her hesitancy. I knew Mom was a true New Yorker. She stayed busy in New York and could easily get around on the subway. In California you have to drive everywhere, and Mom didn't drive anymore.

Adjusting to life without my father was difficult enough. I'm sure she didn't want the extra stress of not being able to come and go as she pleased. She also had a few more years before retirement. She did, however, come out to Los Angeles to visit me every Christmas, and I would go back to Brooklyn to visit her for a few weeks a couple times during the year.

Mom finally retired at sixty-five years old and actually considered going back to school. I thought that was a great idea. She enrolled in college and took a few computer classes and a few writing courses. She really loved it, and we'd discuss all sorts of activities she did at school.

Sometimes she and my sister Debbie would ride up to Atlantic City. Mom seemed to be doing okay. She would never talk about being sad or lonely. For the next couple of years, everything seemed to be fine.

Then it all began to fall apart. Mom started to notice her hands would shake. It was a tremor-like shaking, a little bit at a time and it just happened. She also mentioned that when she tried to walk, her foot got stuck and she couldn't move it. It was as if her mind knew she wanted to walk somewhere, but she had to pause and wait a few seconds later until her foot got the message to move. Her actions were delayed.

"I don't know what it is, Bern," Mom said to me.

I became concerned because Mom had always been so sharp and strong all of her life. Why now, at only sixty-seven, was this happening to her? I really hoped the condition would get better with time and exercise. I didn't want to believe that it was anything serious.

I asked her to go to a doctor and have her symptoms diagnosed and she told me she would. I never inquired as to whether she had gone or not, I just assumed that she did and there was nothing wrong. I thought, if there's something wrong, wouldn't she tell me? I didn't realize it then, but I was in a state of denial. The tremors and shakes Mom experienced in her hands, turned out to be Parkinson's disease.

The point I'd like to make is that when children start to see a decline in a parent as they get older, we tend to not want to accept it. We don't want to face the fact that our parents are not the same as they once were. We remember them as always being so strong, the ones who have it all together. This is common for all children who have ageing parents. Sometimes we think certain conditions just go along with getting older, but this is not always the case.

Many people will do as I did initially, and because of their love and respect for a parent, they will not challenge them about any sickness or symptoms of disease they are experiencing. If their parent tells them they'll handle it and that they'll go to the doctor, the child will let it go at that. We do this because we want our parents to feel that we trust that they still know how to take care of themselves.

Mom was never formally diagnosed with Parkinson's disease. It was not until after she had passed and I did research for this book that I found out she suffered from Parkinson. A year later after her death, while reading some of her writings, the picture became clearer.

Mom possessed great talent as a writer. After reading her works, I came to see her world as deeper and so much more colorful and fascinating than I ever did before. Because Mom dated all of her writings, I could effectively document the progress of her disease. In one of her notebooks she wrote, "I went to the doctor today but I don't think I will tell the children because I don't want them to worry."

I think Mom knew she had Parkinson's disease but chose not to tell us. Mom wanted to protect us from the hurt that we would have experienced had we known her condition. She did protect us for a long while. Sometimes, I now question if certain medications could have controlled that disease. For a while, the Parkinson's seemed to get better and we no longer saw the tremors of her hands or the hesitation of her feet. It all stopped, but did it stop due to the onset of a much worse predator called Alzheimer's?

When Mom turned sixty-eight and had been retired for three years, my brother Kyle needed help a couple of nights during the week with his four little girls; Asia, Paris, Cairo, and Sieana. Kyle was the pastor of a church, his wife the first lady, and their congregation kept them busy. They had to be at church a couple of times during the week, in addition to Sundays. Mom agreed to look after the girls for him.

She had stopped going to school, but didn't seem to mind. She felt quite content taking care of her little granddaughters for the next couple years. But when Mom turned seventy we noticed a big change in her behavior. She was spry and lively at sixty-nine. But at seventy, she seemed so much older to us, just like she had aged considerably over the course of one year.

Mom came out to Los Angeles for Christmas that year, and I noticed she had slowed down even more. Not only did she walk much slower, she had started to become stiff. We thought it was Osteosclerosis, which causes a person to become rigid, until I took her to get a test that came back negative.

Mom continued in her normal everyday routine, then one day she told me that she gave up bingo. I was shocked. She loved bingo. Why did she give it up? She told me because it was difficult for her to keep up with all the numbers. I thought it just might be old age setting in.

Then a couple months later when she was back in New York, a confrontation happened that changed our lives. Mom always called me when she would go out in the evenings, and again when she came back in the house. One Thursday, she had a doctor's appointment at 6:00 p.m. I didn't get a call from her like I usually did, but I didn't think that anything was wrong. I just figured I'd call her early in the morning. But I couldn't rest. My gut told me that something might be wrong. At about 11:00 p.m. California time, which was 2:00 a.m. New York time, I called Mom and she answered.

"Ma, are you alright? Because you didn't call me," I asked.

"I got robbed tonight," she gasped.

I felt like an electric shock had shot through my body.

She explained that she had been walking from the train station and was one block away from home. In November, it was quite dark at 8:30 at night. She said only a few people were out and as she walked down the street, her natural instinct warned her that something just wasn't right; exactly as mine had warned me something wasn't right when I hadn't heard from her.

"You know when you get an initial inclination not to do something?" She asked me.

"Yes, Ma, I know."

"Well, I saw this man down at the end of the block and my first thought was, don't go down that street. I didn't think he wanted to hurt me, but as I kept walking, I felt uneasy. By then I was in the middle of the block, and I didn't want to turn around. What if he came after me? So, I kept walking, again thinking if I don't act afraid he won't hurt me. But even though I reassured myself, I still felt something coming and couldn't do anything about it.

"He'd been on the other side of the street and when he crossed over to my side, that's when I knew I was in trouble. He grabbed my purse, but the way he grabbed it forced me to fall into the gutter and he ran off. I cut my knee but I made it to the house and called the police. I described the man, and before he could get to the train station the cops caught him," Mom explained.

I was elated to hear that her robber had been caught. Mom said she had to go down to the station to identify him. Even although the situation had been rectified, I still worried about Mom. I really think that experience had a devastating affect on her. She didn't go out in the evening alone after that. I soon decided that Mom must come and live with me because I didn't feel it was safe for her to live by herself. I started to talk about it more and more with her, but she still refused to leave New York for good.

Kyle came by and picked Mom up for church during the week, and every Sunday she would go hear him preach, as well. She'd then call and tell me how well he preached. Whenever I returned to New York, I'd always go to hear him. Mom just didn't claim he was good because he was her son. He really is an awesome preacher. Mom would get all of his tapes and when she came to California to visit me, she'd bring them with her. She and I would sit and listen to them, enjoying the word delivered by my brother.

My siblings and I tried to keep Mom busy. She loved to go visit with my sister, Yolanda, who lived in Maryland with her husband Scottie and their two little girls, Olivia and Sophia. Mom took care of Olivia from her birth until she turned a year old. She stayed there in Maryland at Yolanda's house all week, and then she'd come home on the weekends. She'd also visit my sister Debbie and her husband James and their three children: Kirsten, Zeke and Joshua. She saw my brother, Trell, almost every day since he lived so close. His two older children, Little Trell and Sharrell, would often stay with Mom. She remained quite busy with her children and grandchildren.

It was around this time in 2006, when I started to write my first book, *Situations 101*, on relationships. I've always been very interested in how relationships work. I eventually became a relationship coach, and have been of help to many single individuals and couples.

It all began with one lady; I'll call her Lola to protect her privacy. She just didn't understand my advice no matter how many different ways I'd try to tell her. As a result, Lola remained stagnant in her relationship for more than three years. She hadn't made any progress and it frustrated me. I realized that she just dumped her problems on me in order to feel better, but had no real intentions to change her situation.

Then one night at three o'clock, my phone rang. I picked it up and heard Lola crying. I asked her what was wrong.

"I called him, and he won't answer the phone," she said.

"Well, maybe he's asleep. It is three in the morning," I said, hoping the call would be short so I could go back to sleep.

"No, he isn't. Because I called him more than once," she continued.

"How many times have you tried to reach him?" I asked, dreading her answer.

"Over fifteen times!" she admitted.

I knew right then she was overboard and out of control. "Did you leave a message each time?" I asked

"I left so many nasty messages, but now I feel bad for what I said, and he may not speak to me again."

I could only imagine the tone of the messages and that's when it really dawned on me that this girl was in bad shape and needed some serious help. We'd been going back and forth with this same scenario for a little over three years. If she hadn't had enough of the situation, I had. It became obvious to me that she only wanted a sounding board. However, instead of listening to her vent at 3:00 a.m., I decided to write some pointers down for her to read. That way, if she couldn't reach this man in the middle of the night, she wouldn't freak out. She could just read my advice instead of calling me at all hours of the night.

After writing for a while, I realized that I had almost twenty pages of information for her. Those twenty pages eventually turned into my first book, *Situations 101*: Relationships, The Good, The Bad, and The Ugly.

While writing the book I'd call Mom to discuss every situation with her. We spent hours on the phone during the day. I asked her what she thought of the topics that I put into the book.

"If it's true, write it. It will help many people," she advised.

Nothing seemed different in her conversations. We talked as usual, but I couldn't help but wonder what had really been going on with Mom during the last ten years. I knew she had been affected in a very strong way by my father's horrific and untimely death, but Mom never complained. She always seemed so strong and she never wanted us to worry about her. But had depression set in on a very deep level, and we weren't aware of it?

Just because she never talked about depression and never complained, doesn't mean she didn't struggle with some very intense feelings. I knew she missed Dad a lot. He had kept things going for her all of her life. Then all of a sudden it abruptly stopped. Could that have been a big part of why her health declined so much in ten years?

I sensed that Mom had problems right after I finished writing *Situations 101*, and the manuscript had gone to the printer. Mom called me and said she was having a little trouble remembering if she took her high blood pressure pills or not. That sounded quite serious, because missing doses or taking too much medicine can be dangerous. What if she takes too much or not enough? I thought.

I told Mom not to worry. My solution was that we would buy an organizer and, together, while on the phone, we would go over her medication and put each pill and vitamin in each little compartment, one by one. We tried this a few times but Mom said that the process confused her more. That bothered me because Mom had been a bookkeeper and a wonderful organizer; she would never have a problem like this. I had a few weeks free, so I went back to New York to visit her.

When I got to Mom's house, things seemed the same except I had noticed how she didn't put herself together correctly. For example, when we prepared to go out the morning after my arrival in town, she said that she was ready but when I looked at Mommy her hair hadn't been combed right and her clothes didn't match. I didn't say anything that could make her feel like something wasn't right. I didn't want to alarm or embarrass her.

Instead, I said, "Mom, let me do your hair in a cute style."

She agreed, and then I picked out something beautiful and matching for her to wear. I knew then Mommy had to come back home with me so I could keep her together.

"Mom, I want you to come to California with me for a few weeks because I don't want to leave you here by yourself," I casually suggested. Mom was seventy-two; all of her children were grown and even the two grandchildren she lived close to, Sharrell and Little Trell, were off at college.

She finally agreed. "I'll go for a few weeks, Bern, but I can't stay there but a short while. I don't want to leave my home empty too long."

I assured her that she'd only be gone a couple of weeks or so.

While Mom stayed with me, things seemed fine except the slight tremor in her hands had returned. Other than that she seemed okay. Then I noticed that her thought patterns seemed rather incoherent.

"I have to pay my bills, Bern," she would say. "Where is my purse?" But her purse was right next to her. This went on for a few weeks and finally she wanted to go back home. That seemed to be her only concern, getting back to her house.

I took her back to New York after about a month, and once at home, she appeared to be at peace, no longer asking me about her personal belongings. We had been there for about two weeks, when one day I went to the store and within a half-hour Mom called me on her cell phone. She had us all on speed dial, making it easy to reach any one of her children and grandchildren.

"Bern, I'm scared. Something is not right. I'm really scared," she said.

"Mom, what do you mean?" I asked. "Is something in the house scaring you?"

"No, but something is wrong with me and I'm scared," she said. "I don't know what it is, Bern, but I can feel it. Something's wrong."

"I'll be back soon, Mom. Everything will be okay. I am on my way back now," I said.

Less than five minutes later she called me again. "I don't know what's going on but I'm scared," she repeated.

A wave of panic washed over me. I rushed back, and when I got to her door and knocked, I could hear her calling out to me.

"I fell, Bern," she yelled.

I got my key out and unlocked the door. When I rushed into the house, I saw Mom sprawled out on the floor, lying very still.

"Ma, what happened?" I asked as I tried to help her up.

"I lost my balance and fell, but I couldn't get up because I had nothing to hold on to," she gasped.

She had fallen in the living room, right in the middle of the floor, and there was nothing around for her to grab onto and pull herself up. I was afraid. What if I hadn't taken my keys with me because I was just going to the store? Thank God I was able to come to her rescue.

After I got Mom up, I took her to the bathroom to see if she had hit her head or had broken anything. I was very concerned because I planned to return to California the next day. I was supposed to leave Mom at her home alone because that's what she wanted and would make her happy. I wanted to make her happy but I had to take action.

"That's it, Mom. You're coming back with me," I said. "What if you had fallen after I left for California? Mom, you're coming back with me. You cannot be here by yourself anymore. I am not leaving you here. You are coming to live with me from now on, do you understand, Mom"? I felt my mom's silence and what might be going on with her feelings, and in her heart and mind. She may have been a bit confused but my heart melted into her feelings and I grabbed her little face and said, "You are with me Ma. We are going to be together always from now on. Wherever I go, you go. You will never be alone again, not ever, okay Ma?"

"Okay," she said.

I held her and said, "I love you Mommy." I felt something had changed in Mom's brain that day and she knew it too. I believe the brain was making another shift and she felt it happening in her head. Like anyone she became afraid. That must have been a terrible feeling because she had told me in her phone call that she was scared.

I then grabbed Mommy in my arms and cried like a baby for her. She cried too and we said nothing, not one word. But it was the moment that we realized it was a shift in our lives and our position in our lives, forever. She became my baby to take care of her like she had taken care of me as my mother. I knew what I had to be for her.

"We will come back to your home as often as you like but you are with me now." That was that. I made the decision and Mom appeared to be okay with it.

"I would never feel right if you stayed here and I didn't take you with me." I felt a little additional explanation wouldn't hurt. "You are with me always, from now on. Okay Mom?"

"Okay," she said.

I held her and said, "I love you, Mom. I love you so much."

Something had changed in Mom's mind and that day she knew it, too. I believe she felt her brain changing and became afraid. I held her in my arms and cried like a baby for her. She cried too, but we said nothing.

That afternoon the fear for my mother's life was born and it grew and remained in the pit of my soul, until my mother's last breath.

Back in California, I made an appointment within the same week to go see a neurologist.

We went in and the doctor did some tests.

"Can you help me?" Mom asked the doctor.

"What can be done to get my mom well again?" I asked him as he brought us back into his office.

"I am going to give your mom Aricept. It's a medication for what your mom has. She has Alzheimer's," the doctor said.

Not knowing a single thing about Alzheimer's, I asked the doctor, "Will this medicine cure it?"

He looked at me, then looked down and shook his head no. He had a bottle of Aricept there in his office and gave it to us. "This medicine will slow the disease down. When you get home give her one pill. I am going to write a prescription for her. Does she have good insurance, because this medication is quite expensive," the doctor said. The Aricept cost $160.00 for 30 tablets without insurance, and that was the cost of the lowest dose.

"Yes, she has Blue Cross Insurance," I told him.

"Good for you. I'm putting her on a low dosage because she is in the early stages now. This is a progressive disease and there is no cure for it," the doctor said.

"Well, I am going to do everything I can to find one," I told him.

The doctor looked at me and gave me a half-smile. "I'd like to see her back here in a month, okay?"

"Sure," I said, determined to show him that Mommy would be getting better from this disease he called Alzheimer's.

When we got out of there I was sort of angry with the doctor. I felt like he acted as though it was hopeless. I turned to Mommy and said, "He don't know us, huh, Mom? We fought through many other things in life and we will fight through this, too. Mom, you are going to be cured from this thing, you watch. With your faith and my determination, God has never let us down yet." And with every fiber in my body no one could tell me that Mommy was not going to be cured from this disease.

When we got home I gave her the Aricept. Within a half-hour, Mommy said the cutest thing to me. She was sitting in front of the television, and said, "Bern, I'm back."

"Really, Mom? You feel like you're back to yourself?" I asked. She nodded yes. It seemed that the Aricept medicine made her thinking clearer almost immediately.

I called my brothers and sisters and told them that Mommy had a disease called Alzheimer's. They didn't know anything about the disease either. I told them the doctor gave her some medicine and that she was doing better. Then I started to read up on Alzheimer's.

Everywhere I turned to get information the facts were the same: no cure found. It was unbelievable. If they could slow the disease down, why couldn't they stop it? There just had to be a cure somewhere, somehow. I just had to find it, that's all.

I remained determined but I still had so many questions. Yes, Mom had kept busy for many years, but what was really going on in her heart about her life? Had she been in a quiet depression? Was she lonely for a life that she and Dad had imagined they'd have after retirement? They were so looking forward to that time in their lives. Did depression cause her Alzheimer's, or did the shock of my father's murder cause the onset of the disease? Did nerve damage bring on Parkinson's disease before the Alzheimer's, or could it have been the Alzheimer's that was gradually coming on and triggering the Parkinson's?

These serious questions remain unanswered now, but I pray that there is a breakthrough soon that can answer them, for me and many others, who have suffered as I have from this monster of the mind called Alzheimer's.

7.

The Beginning of My Caregiving Journey

I am not a martyr, just a daughter who loved her mother more than words can say. Please keep in mind the changes that affected my mom during her suffering with Alzheimer's were caused by the disease. It is not the person, but the disease that causes them to behave the way they do. My heart still feels pain for her, even as I share these words with you now.

My experience as my mother's caregiver was one of my greatest gifts. Mom always said if she ever had to live with someone when she got older, she wanted to live with me. I always said I was ready for it whenever that day came. So, I considered myself blessed when that day did come. I was prepared for her to be with me. It didn't matter that she suffered from a dreadful sickness; it only mattered that I now had my best friend with me every day.

But the care-giving journey threw me into a whirlwind that forced me to grow up in a staggering moment. Before the change, I still felt like my mother's little girl. Even though being a good and grown lady with two daughters of my own, I still felt mothered and protected like little girls do. Now the roles had reversed and it was my turn to nurture and protect my mother.

When Mom came to live with us, my baby daughter, Brittany Rose, was only eight years old. It was quite a transition for Brittany because I had to give Mom so much attention, and she found it very difficult to see her grandmother needing so much help. Since I had to split my attention between them, naturally my daughter felt a tinge of jealousy.

"Why would anyone be jealous of me? Look at me. No one wants to be like this," Mom said to me.

"Mom, Brittany will grow to understand in a little while," I said. I hurt for my mom, and I knew that I would have to really work with Brittany to help her understand her grandmother's condition. It was new to all of us. At this point none of us knew what this disease was about to do. We were learning as we went along.

Even though Mommy had been diagnosed with Alzheimer's, I still launched the promotion of my book, *Situations101*. This was not only my book, but it belonged to Mommy as well. I always felt like she co-authored it.

The time came for me to start touring, so it was perfect having Mom with me. I took her on the road to every book signing, conference and speaking engagement. I never left her behind. Most times I had Brittany too, because my appearances occurred on the weekends. But if I had to leave on a Wednesday or Thursday, Brittany would stay back home with my older daughter, Dior Ravél. Dior was only eighteen years old herself, but very responsible and she took excellent care of Brittany.

While on the road, I'd dress Mom so beautifully and she always received wonderful compliments from everyone. Mom would sit to the right of me and my fans would greet her and show her so much love.

"Bern, they really love you," she said to me one day as she observed my fans.

We met many friends, some who would write to Mom often, offering her wonderful words of love and encouragement.

They'd send her beautiful cards that I would put around her room. All of this support served as inspiration to both of us. Mom appeared to be extremely happy, and it gave me great joy to see her experience this love. It was, I feel, a great reward for all of the hard work that she put into helping me to achieve a name the whole world had come to know.

It reminded me of when I was that ten-year-old little girl, and Mom said, "Bern, one day the whole world is going to know your name."

I often wondered how Mom knew it would turn out just like she predicted. I guess that's what having faith is all about. Then she put action behind her faith and it came to pass. Mom was a very special lady in this world. I have always felt she had favor throughout her life. She loved God so much and God loved her.

In the beginning of my mother's diagnosis with Alzheimer's, I thought it was a disease that could be fixed with a change of diet and vitamins. That's how little I knew about it. Like many people, I lingered in a state of denial that my mother was in the grip of this monster that would eventually take her life.

"How can this disease have so much power?" I asked myself, until I learned the devastating affects of Alzheimer's on the individual person. It has the power to do with its victims as it will, because there is no cure, and we don't know exactly where it comes from. With this reality check constantly on my mind, as I so desperately tried to save my mother's life, it made our fight much more difficult. I felt the impact of this disease chasing us. As soon as I got a handle on one stage of its debilitating damage and made the adjustments, we were thrown into another stage that brought with it new challenges.

I cried and cried at night. This was the most difficult time for me. I cried so much I felt an ache in my mind, my heart and stomach. I cried for hours at night searching for answers, pleading with God, just crying until my eyes were swollen shut. It shouldn't have been like this at all.

Finally, I made the deliberate decision to just enjoy my mom every day we still had together. I got Mom up every morning with the brightest smile and acted as if nothing was wrong at all. My determination was steadfast not to let this disease take our joy from us. That was my only way to fight back. Alzheimer's would not rob my mother of her ability to live the loving, wonderful and happy life that she so richly deserved. We lived in the moment of every single day.

This period provided some of our family's greatest times with Mom. I could see that she was happy and peaceful, free to be her beautiful self, surrounded with laughter and love. What I witnessed and realized was one of God's miracles. Mom was now showing me how to live in the moment and see the beauty in all things, like in a simple rose if only we take time to look at it and see its beauty. This became my fulfillment, and the only way I could fight back was by living each day to the fullest.

When I got Mom dressed with her hair and makeup done, I could see that she loved it. She looked pretty and felt pretty. We had a cute joke between us. Sometimes she would call me mama and I would respond by saying,

"Okay, that's fair. You were my mama, now it's my turn to be your mama." She would just smile, then I would give her a big hug and whisper in her ear, "But you know you're my mama, right?"

She would nod her head yes, and smile.

My mother always saw the good in people and the beauty in things before Alzheimer's and the diagnosis didn't change that, because now she was able to stop and smell the roses, too. She would tell me that something was pretty, and when I looked at what she was talking about, it really was pretty.

I began to observe the slow decline of Mom's condition in the early stages of the disease, and to feel the drain of death easing its way into my heart and creeping onto my mother. I shook it off. I just couldn't accept this fate. I refused to stop looking, asking for help everywhere I could. But no one could give me the answer I sought: the cure.

I continued to give Mom vitamins. I had a physical therapist come to my home to keep her moving and strong. But slowly, Mom moved into another stage of this disease, and I feared that I wouldn't find a cure in time to save her. But I never stopped praying and asking God to help us. And Mommy's faith remained as strong as ever. We prayed every day.

But it seemed that each day it became more difficult for me to breathe. I had to face the painful reality that Alzheimer's would not leave our lives. I felt hopeless so many times. I cried at night. It shouldn't be like this. Mom and I were supposed to be having the time of our lives now, traveling the country and promoting my book. Why God why, I wondered so many times. But God slowly gave me the grace to handle what I most dreaded.

Mom stayed on Aricept, which worked well for her. The medication slowed the Alzheimer's down and allowed Mom to focus quite a bit. But we still had moments when, despite the medication, Alzheimer's would rear its ugly head. Many times in my mother's early stages in her battle with

Alzheimer's, we would pull up to my home and she would ask, "Who lives here?"

Once during the early stages of Alzheimer's, Mom accompanied me to D.C. for an interview on the Donny Simpson Radio Show. The night before, I always helped give Mom her shower to make it easier for me in the mornings. That morning, I got up at 6:00 a.m., I got her up, helped her brush her teeth, washed her face, fixed her hair and fed her, all by 7:15 a.m. Then I got myself together. We were ready for the car to pick us up by 8:15 a.m., all done up and on time.

We arrived at the station and just before I had to go on the air, Mom's nose began to bleed. It frightened me because I had no idea what caused the bleeding. There happened to be a policeman at the station, and he said to get some ice and put it on her top lip to stop the bleeding. We did that and it worked. Then, they called me in to go on the air.

The interview went well, but my nerves and emotions were a mess. Afterwards, I called Mom's doctor and he said she would be okay, but to have her lie down for a while. We went back to the hotel and rested for a few hours. Mom felt fine but it really scared me. I asked her doctor if I should continue to take her with me on the road, and he said absolutely if I wanted to and if Mom wanted to go.

I continued to travel with Mom and her condition seemed to be back to normal. But once we returned home, she woke up one morning and would not open her eyes. She kept them closed all day. Everyone tried to make her open them but she wouldn't do it.

"My eyes are open," she insisted.

"Mom, look at television," I said, hoping that would get her to open her eyes.

"I am looking at television," she replied. She actually thought that she was watching TV.

When Brittany came home from school at 3:00 p.m., she went over to Mom and said,

"Mama, open your eyes."

Mom's eyelids fluttered open with the sound of Brittany's voice. But that made me even more concerned, because the changes Mom experienced came much more rapidly and so unpredictable.

During this mild stage, I'd take Mom to the mall at least once a week. One afternoon, Mom, Brittany and I passed by Lady Foot Locker, and Brittany wanted a pair of shoes that cost about a hundred dollars. Mom went into her purse and gave Brittany a hundred dollar bill. That girl of mine was so thrilled and surprised, and when she went and got those shoes, it made her the happiest little girl ever.

Then we went for ice cream and this young guy, about 19 years old, didn't have enough money to pay for his ice cream. Mom came to his rescue. She pulled a ten dollar bill out of her purse and gave it to him. At first he didn't want to take it, but he eventually did. I asked Mom why she gave the young man that money.

"Because he's young, and he's trying to make it. He just wanted some ice cream," she said.

I'd also take Mom to get her hair done once a week, and the lady who did her hair had five children. When it was time to pay, Mom gave her the amount it cost for her hair, and then pulled out a tip of forty dollars, sometimes even more. I asked Mom why she gave the beautician such a large tip.

"She needs help Bern, because she has so many children," she again replied.

"That was very nice, Mom," I said.

I didn't want to tell her she shouldn't have done that, because her reasons for doing so were good ones. She gave from her heart. But I didn't want other people who didn't understand my mother's kind heart to take advantage of her generosity.

Sometime later that year, I started to notice that Mom would misplace her money. I immediately realized I had to do something to protect her finances. With great hesitation and sadness, I went to Toys-R-Us and bought some play money. As I replaced the real money with the play money, it brought tears to my eyes because Mom had been the best bookkeeper, and she used to handle money so well. She didn't even recognize that the money wasn't real. When she looked in her purse and saw the play money, she smiled.

I went into the bathroom and broke down and cried. The death reaper, Alzheimer's, was taking another part of Mom away from her. The hurt and anger at this disease rose up within me, once more. I found it extremely difficult to accept that Mom no longer realized the difference between the money.

I had to replace Mom's jewelry with costume jewelry. One day she went to the park with the nurse I'd hired to help out part-time, and she had on a beautiful ruby and diamond ring. When they came back from the park she no longer had it on. I couldn't blame anyone because she might have taken it off and dropped it. I didn't think to remove it, even though a few weeks earlier she lost her mother's ring that she wore and never took off. I noticed it missing one day when I looked at her hand.

These are some of the signs no one tells you to look out for when you are caring for your loved one with Alzheimer's.

If I had known to look out for something like this earlier, I would have replaced her rings long before she lost two very valuable ones.

A couple weeks later, I realized that I had to take her ID and insurance cards away from her as well. She'd take them out of her purse, and I'd find them on the floor. She knew that she had the cards but couldn't remember where she put them. She asked me over and over about these cards. I told her that I would hold them for her.

She said, "No. I want my cards, Bern."

I realized I had to do something so she wouldn't lose them. I made copies of all her cards and had them laminated. That made them look authentic. I gave her the laminated copies, and I kept the real ones. She didn't notice that they weren't the original cards. She was satisfied to have her cards back again. To realize that she couldn't tell the difference made me accept that the Alzheimer's was slowly capturing more of Mom's life. More of her was slipping away.

I couldn't stop crying that day. My mom grabbed my hand and said, "Don't be sad, Bern."

I looked at her and tried to dry my eyes, I then hugged her because I needed Mom to hug me. Oh, how I needed her to hug me.

If only I had known more about Alzheimer's and had recognized its symptoms, I would have taken Mom to the doctor right away. Then she would have been prescribed the Aricept at the very first signs of Alzheimer's. It would have at least slowed the disease down at the earliest possible time.

As Mom moved into the moderate stage of the disease, it began to affect us in even more ways. Whenever she sat in the living room, there were a few times she claimed that she saw babies.

"Watch out for the baby," she said.

I would make light of the situation and say, "Okay Mom, where's the baby 'cause we don't want to step on it?"

That seemed to satisfy her concern for the infants she believed she saw. My husband and I would always make things as light and easy as possible, so that life would be as normal for her as possible. If she saw babies we would ask where she saw them, and we would act as if that was normal because it was normal for her.

The nights began to get more difficult to deal with because she started to walk around. This late night confusion, wandering and pacing is commonly known as "sun downing." She'd forget the location of rooms in the house. Since Mom used to sleep with me. She'd wake me up several times a night and ask for directions to the bathroom. This caused problems for me, because over the period of a year it severely interrupted my sleep pattern, and I stayed awake most of the night. I did my best to function on the few hours of sleep that I could manage.

Mom scared us because she was such a quiet person and no one ever heard her move around. We wouldn't know she'd gotten out of the bed until she tapped us on the shoulder to wake us up. I thought that I might get little bells and tie them on her clothes so that if she got up, her movements would jingle the bells. But I never had to do that because Mom did listen to me. I would tell her not to get up at night because she could hurt herself. She stopped the wandering after that. She would wait until morning when I woke her up to start the day.

I was pleased to know that Mom did understand that getting up alone could be dangerous for her. I'd already moved all of the furniture a few months earlier, because I didn't want her to stumble and fall on anything that could hurt her. I had to move all objects that could harm her, and put them away so that she would be safe around the house.

At this stage in Mom's disease she began to remember more of her younger years rather than connecting with the present. Many people with Alzheimer's remember an earlier part of their lives that have good memories for them. Mom especially focused on her teenage years. She called for her Aunt Rena a few times, but Rena had been dead for many years, a fact that she had forgotten. I told Mom not to call her, because she had passed away. She listened to me and stopped.

There was, however, a fun part to all of this remembering the past. I'd show Mom her junior high school graduation picture, and she'd light up with the biggest, prettiest smile. I'd ask her if she remembered a few of her classmates and she did remember them. She talked about Shirley, Jerri and Annie Carrol, her close friends in school, and she'd point to this one boy named Buddy Willis. When I asked her about him, she said he used to like her when they were fourteen years old. I think she liked him too, because a smile always crossed her face when we talked about him. This was a great way for us to connect. She and I talked about those days almost every day like a comforting bedtime story. It made her extremely happy.

In 2009, still during this stage, Mom and I traveled to one of my book signings in Chicago. We had just settled into our hotel room and relaxed for about an hour. We then made our way into the bathroom and I helped as she washed her face. Suddenly, she seemed as though she was dizzy and on the verge of passing out. I took her by the arms and got her back to the bed. I then called the paramedics.

When they rushed into the room, I shouted. "Be careful with her, she has Alzheimer's."

The medic did a cursory examination, then stared up at me and replied. "Ma'am, your mother does not need to go to the hospital."

A very curious and surprised expression crept all over my face. "What?"

The medic ignored my response, looked at Mom and asked. "Who is the President of the United States?"

Mom smiled at the medics as she struggled to remember the President's name.

The medic prompted her. "Well, is he black or white?"

"He's black, and he's cute, too." With her response, we all laughed and Mom did too.

One of the last events I took Mom to was the Mayor's Masked Ball in Atlanta. We had attended the event a couple of times before and she always had a good time. That night, during the ball I noticed how her movements became slow and she didn't want to stay and enjoy the festivities. I believe the costumes and masks confused her, so we left the ball and spent a quiet night upstairs in our room.

We continued to travel to my speaking engagements, but it now took more than one hour to get her ready for the day. Her movements became much slower, and traveling a burden because it took us longer to get ready.

One evening when I was putting Mom to bed she said, "Thank you."

"Oh Mom, you don't have to thank me," I said. "You would do this for me."

I realized how much she appreciated what I did for her. Then there were times when she would just look at me and smile. I knew that her silent smile meant thank you. She really was the sweetest of all ladies, and her spirit truly so beautiful.

It was bittersweet when our travels finally came to an end. We'd had so much fun, met so many people and recorded so many great memories.

I took Mom to the adult day care center three times a week. She seemed to enjoy seeing all the other seniors. They played music and danced. Mom and I would sit and watch. The center always had a variety of activities going on. Mom participated in the ones that she could, but just being there and around all the fun made her so happy.

Mom began to eat less and eat slower, and at first it caused me a great deal of concern. Rapid weight loss can be a symptom of cancer, but tests came back negative. Thank God! Still, the weight continued to fall away from her body. She was now a size 10 when she had been a size 14–16 before the weight loss. She eventually stabilized at a size six.

Mom also stopped swallowing her medication. She just held the pills in her mouth and then took them out and put them in her napkins. I knew Mom loved vanilla ice cream, so I got the idea to crush up some of her medications and slip them into her bowl. She would eat all of her ice cream and, therefore, get all of her medications she needed every day. I made sure she ate as much as she liked. It made me happy to see her eating and enjoying her ice cream, and it relieved me to know that this way she would get the medicine also.

Towards the end of this stage, Mom started to slow down

even more. It used to take me an hour to get her ready for the day but now it took two hours. After I'd get her ready for the day, she'd sit in front of the television and watch The Maury Povich Show. After an hour or so of that, I'd give her a pen and paper and ask her to write her name. She managed to write parts of it but after a while she'd stop.

I kept an album of pictures right next to her, and we looked through it every day. I'd show her pictures of my dad, her mom and dad and pictures of my siblings. It allowed her to remain connected to her life. She was always so happy when she looked at pictures of her loved ones. I would also show her the pretty cards friends would send her.

When Mom wanted to listen to music, I played Calypso and Salsa, the same music she listened to as a young girl. It always seemed to make her happy. I'd get her up from the chair and we'd dance. I'd hold her, as we swayed back and forth to the music.

Even though she was a little thinner, Mom remained healthy and still looked beautiful, not like anything was wrong with her at all. But the Alzheimer's was there and eventually, from time to time, she got this look on her face called "the mask." It was a distant look in her eyes, with very little expression on her face. But Mom never forgot us because we were with her every day, interacting with her. I considered it a blessing that part of her brain hadn't been affected.

During the final stages of the disease I began to realize the affect that Alzheimer's had on me as the sole caregiver for Mom. I gave her more of my time because she needed that to stay alive. Mom began clinging to me, and I knew she was afraid to be left without me. So, I kept her with me.

I never made time for myself, and I spent no time with friends. I worried, always on edge. I'd never leave Mom for long because I felt guilty going out and enjoying any personal time. I figured that even if I went out I'd be worrying the entire evening, so why bother?

My sleep was disrupted by constant concern about one thing or another, my health was failing, and my diet was terrible. I stopped going to the gym and I no longer exercised on a regular routine. I gained weight, my blood pressure had gone up and I was not feeling well. But I didn't really care, because my concern was only to help my mom stay alive as long as I could.

I felt like the disease constantly chased Mom and me. As soon as I got a handle on one new change, along came another. Her condition changed so fast, that I knew Alzheimer's was nearing its final stages and the damage became quite vivid to the eye. In hindsight, I knew that I had become depressed. Eventually, I went to the doctor because I realized that if I didn't take better care of myself I could get into trouble with my health, and it could be serious. That is why it is very important for caregivers to take care of themselves when they care for a loved one, so that they don't get sick.

I got a handle on my physical health, but there were still emotional aspects I needed to take care of. Unfortunately, those aspects weren't always predictable or preventable. One day Mom and I sat in the den watching *Good Times* and my character, Thelma, was in one of her perpetual fights with J.J.

Mom looked over at me and said, "That's a cute little girl." She no longer recognized her daughter as that little girl, Thelma.

Feeling rather dejected I replied. "Yes, Mom, she is cute."

Inside, I felt like someone twisted a knife in my heart. This monster of the mind called Alzheimer's had taken away from my mother, the very memory of me being on *Good Times*, an accomplishment that had changed our lives, and had brought so much pride to my mother. If it hadn't been for Mom I would never have been on the show.

Now, Alzheimer's had taken that precious memory away from her. Right at that moment, I made up my mind to do whatever possible to fight against this disease by traveling around the nation and exposing this monster through education and awareness. That's why I formed a foundation in Mom's honor and called it "Remembering the Good Times" an Alzheimer's Foundation.

With renewed determination, I stayed on the Internet night and day, hoping for some miracle. I read about coconut oil helping with Alzheimer's, so I gave Mom a tablespoon of coconut oil in her oatmeal every day. I did see some improvement in how well she focused. That lasted for a few months but the disease still had its way and pulled Mom further down into its hell, and pushed me into deeper despair.

My saving grace was that, although Mom slowly lost her ability to do more and more physically, she did not lose her understanding of what happened around her. Although at this late stage of Alzheimer's, Mom no longer initiated conversations, she answered question I asked her with simple words or short sentences and, therefore, responded appropriately.

I never knew what might happen to Mom at any time because the disease caused changes so rapidly. Although I read about the stages of Alzheimer's and what to expect at any time, I still fought for her life and still hoped to defy the odds.

Mom continued to slow down even more, and now she no longer walked very much. A physical therapist came to the house three times a week to exercise and walk and keep her body moving. I also had to consider a nurse coming into my home on a more permanent basis. We faced the task of interviewing many nurses and caregivers. That was another turning point for us. I hadn't left Mom with anyone other than family. I found it very hard, to let someone take care of Mom for two or three days, without me.

I chose a very lovely nurse and caregiver for Mom, and they took good care of her. I considered myself lucky to have found them, because this could have been a challenging process. But during this stage, Mom did not want me to leave her at all. She wanted me there with her 24/7. What did make me feel better about leaving Mom, was the fact that my daughters would be home when I had to leave the house. With me gone, they assisted the nurse in caring for Mom.

When I first began to leave her with the nurse, I knew she was being well cared for, and I felt at ease. I constantly had Mom on my mind while out there working. I needed to know how she was doing at all times, and called home to speak to her and the caregiver every few hours. It turned out just fine; Mom really liked the nurses. They provided the relief I needed to go do my job without worry, and when I came back home everything was good and Mom appeared happy.

When I didn't travel, we got up every day and I'd dress Mom, and make her look as pretty as ever. I bought her some puzzles so that we could sit and put them together while we watched TV. On certain days, Mom would be much more alert and active than other days. During the latter part of this stage, Mom wanted to lie down a lot; she said she felt tired most of the time. We had to make sure Mom turned over every two hours while in bed, to avoid forming any pressure sores from lying in one spot for too long.

At night when I prepared Mom for bed, I talked to her and read the Bible to her and we'd say our prayers. She always said the entire "Our Father" prayer with me every night. Then I'd kiss her goodnight, and she'd go off to sleep.

I tried to keep Mom as busy as I could, so I enrolled her in a water coloring class. Mom was losing her ability to paint objects in a realistic form, but her paintings were sweet, little and colorful images on her canvas. They were beautiful to me, and I'd tell her that she did a good job. She beamed with pride and that brought joy to my heart.

Allow me to share something very special with you, and what I'm about to tell you is the absolute truth. Angels are real and they really do surround special people. From the very time Mom came to live with me, I believed that she brought an angel with her who diligently watched over her.

One day, while she sat in her favorite chair in her bedroom watching television, I stood next to her and smelled this beautiful, fragrant aroma. It was a very sweet scent, one I had never smelled before.

"Ma, do you smell that? You brought an angel with you when you came here, Mom," I said. I'd heard that when angels are around, you may not always see them but you can hear them in a beautiful sound or smell them in a beautiful scent.

"No, I can't smell that," Mom said. I then remembered that Mom had told me she couldn't smell things anymore. One of the first senses to go when someone is diagnosed with Alzheimer's is their sense of smell.

"Well, your angel is here," I said.

About three months later, while in the kitchen and Mom still in her bedroom sitting in the same spot, I heard her soft voice call my name.

"Bern?"

"Yes, Mom?" I replied.

"I smell the angel," she said.

I quickly walked toward the bedroom, but on my way there I thought, how is that she can smell anything.

But when I walked into the room I caught the aroma of that beautiful sweet smell of the angel. And I smiled. "Yes, Mom. Your angel is here." God allowed her to feel and to know that she had an angel with her. God is so good. It was a miracle and it couldn't have come at a better time.

Just before Christmas of 2010, I got an overwhelming desire to take pictures of Mom and our family. I called a photography studio and made an appointment for us. Somehow, I knew that would be the last time we'd be able to take such pictures.

My brothers, and sisters regularly came out to visit Ma. She enjoyed that, and despite her Alzheimer's, was always aware that she had five children. She would often say to me,

"You know I have other children."

"Yes Ma, I know you do." And then we talked about each one of them.

"Trell and I are buddies," Mom said.

"You know Kyle is a true preacher. He is for real," she said about her son.

"Yes, Mom, I know he is."

"I talked to Debbie the other day," Mom continued.

"Yes, you did, Mom." I felt elated that she remembered because she had spoken with her a few days earlier.

"And today is Yolanda's birthday," she informed me. My rejoicing deep inside continued. Mom had it right. I was amazed at the surprising number of facts Mom remebered even in the grip of Alzheimer's.

When my nephew, Little Trell, had come to visit Mom a few weeks earlier she'd said, "My boy came to see me." She'd always called him, her boy.

Trell had traveled from New York to California to see his mama. Then Sharrell, or as Mom called her, her little girl, came to visit. Mom had always been very close to the two of them because she'd helped to raise them.

"Yes Mom, she came to see you."

I'd show Mom pictures of all of her grandchildren and great-grandchildren. She just looked at them and smiled. It made me so happy to know that she hadn't forgotten the people who'd meant so much to her. But Mom retaining bits and pieces of her memory was bittersweet. She would also say,

"I want Greg. That's my husband."

"Yes, Ma, I know." Even though I missed my father so much and I knew Mom did also, we still smiled.

8.

THE FACILITY

Mom's final downfall began when in March 2011, she woke up one morning to an extremely swollen face. One of her eyes appeared red, redder than a normally irritated or infected eye. By mid-morning, the swelling had gotten worse. I called the ambulance and we rushed Mom to the hospital.

The diagnosis revealed that Mom had shingles. The doctors told me they could treat the viral infection and eventually she would be strong enough to come home. The doctors also advised that she get a feeding tube because she wasn't eating very well at this time. She had stopped chewing her food and didn't swallow at all.

Mom's doctor advised us to send her to a respite hospital. Her frail condition prevented her from going home, but she also wasn't sick enough to stay in the hospital. I looked at several places and asked a lot of questions. Since I had Mom's power of attorney, I could make the final decision. It is important that every caregiver have power of attorney so they can make the best physically related and financial decisions for their loved one, when they are no longer able to make them. The power of attorney should be executed while the patient still understands what they are signing.

I found several places with five-star ratings, and ultimately chose the facility that I thought best for her. The hospital staff had referred it to me. The facility appeared to be flawless on paper, and when I went to visit with them, the actual facility looked like a suitable place for Mom to recuperate.

However, from what I've since learned, I will give you this advice: if you ever have to put a loved one into one of those facilities, understand that there may be many that aren't what they appear to be or what they say they are on paper. When you go to visit and speak with the staff, they may put up a front for the family that doesn't reflect who they really are at all. They may hide from the family, desperately searching for the best place to put their loved one, who they really are and what they do or don't do. Unfortunately, a family may not ever see through this facade until it is too late.

Within one week of moving Mom to this respite hospital, she caught a C.difficile bacterial infection. I didn't know what caused the infection, but I have since learned that it is passed on to patients when the staff does not follow proper hygiene protocols, like hand washing. This was a devastating as well as preventable development, since Mom's system did not need the additional illness.

I thought Mom would be out of there within two weeks. Now, she had to be put on antibiotics for one month. They had to monitor her condition because the antibiotics could destroy some of the normal, helpful bacteria as well as the bacteria causing this illness. The doctors informed me that I could not take her out of the facility, because a C.difficile bacterial infection is very contagious. I had to leave Mom there until her infection cleared up.

During her extended stay, I started to observe the way the staff at this facility handled their patients. The nurse's aides caring for the patients would not use soap to clean them. They would just use water in a basin and wring the water over the patient, then wipe them dry. I concluded that is how Mom caught the nasty infection, that weakened her immune system even further.

I stayed with Mom most of the day, but at night they made the family members leave. One morning I went over to the facility earlier than normal and found Mother lying half way off the bed with no sheet, and she hadn't been cleaned up. I was livid and boy did they hear from me! I had been looking for another place for Mom ever since she caught the bacterial infection. I complained, however, my priority was to get Mom out of there and into a reliable, responsible, safe and trustworthy place.

It was really horrific for me when I recognized the deplorable condition of that facility, when they had initially put up such a flawless front. One would think it was the absolute perfect place to leave your loved one. The facility charged me $2,000 per month out of pocket, and I found out that they charged Mom's insurance up to $8,000 per month: a total of $10,000. But Mom did not get the care she needed. I would have paid whatever to get my mother the best of care, as I am sure most families would.

I believe there are good and decent facilities out there that live up to their reputation. Then, there are those that fail miserably. The sad thing is you don't know which ones are which if you can't trust their ratings on paper and what they show you when making an initial visit. It's the bad ones who fail to live up to standard practices of the industry and always want more money than they deserve. These greedy ones are giving a bad name to facilities everywhere.

Once it was safe to do so, I had Mom removed and placed

in another home, much better than the first one. But allow me to offer this advice; no matter how good the reputation the facility might have, it seems that some workers will undoubtedly take the easiest and quickest way of cleaning the patients—using just water and no soap. In Mom's case, the infection left her body, but it returned three more times, resulting in her having to take more and more antibiotics. Once you get the bacterial infection, sometimes it goes away but will return. My research has found that this is the cause of many patients dying in these facilities.

When a caregiver is faced with extremely difficult choices to make on behalf of their loved one, they rely on professionals to tell them the truth and to be honest so the correct decisions can be made. What I thought would be a two-week stay, ended up lasting six months and ended with my Mom's death.

I kept Mom home with me for eight years. If I had the choice, she would have stayed there, in the room that she loved. I would have never put her into one of those facilities if I didn't have to, but in Mom's case I was advised to do so by her doctors because she needed special care of the feeding tube. It also would have been fine for Mom to be in one of those places to regain her strength, if the facility had lived up to its five-star rating.

If you can keep your loved one at home, please do so for as long as you can. Even if a respite hospital has high ratings on paper, it can be deceiving. Sometimes these facilities pass the state audit because they know when the auditors are coming. They clean up the surroundings and make the environment perfect for the auditor's evaluation, resulting in a five-star report at that time. After they receive their report or their five-star rating, they return back to their normal, sub-standard operating procedures.

That particular facility puts on a good front for the families. They told us all of the activities they had and that they would be doing this and that for the patients, but they didn't always do what they promised. Sometimes the patients just lie there until someone comes to visit them, and the planned activities never happened.

Mom had a private nurse to sit with her whenever I was not there. Some patients had family members and people from their church, that rotated and sat with them. It's just a good idea to be there for your loved one as much as possible when they spend time in these types of facilities. It shows the staff that if something is not right, you will be there to notice.

The most sickening aspect of this entire situation, my Mom was aware of a lot more than people thought. She knew what was going on around her, but the Alzheimer's rendered her powerless to protest the treatment she received

Mom had been in the second facility for about a month. Even though she would speak to me, Mom hadn't said a word to any of the nurses and they hadn't heard her voice. One day a nurse came in while I sat in the chair next to Mom's bed. The nurse had to change something on Mom and I guess she was a little rough.

"Don't hurt me," Mom said.

The nurse jerked back. "Oh, you can talk?" she asked.

"Yes, she can talk," I said and laughed.

Once the nurse left the room, Mom and I laughed, but soon my tone became more serious. "Mom, you tell me if they do anything to you, okay?"

Mom smiled and said, "Yeah, I will."

The night of Saturday, September 3, 2011, I dreamt that my Mom died. When I woke up, I was practically in shock because at this point she seemed to be doing just fine in the nursing home. In fact, I thought she'd be able to come home the next weekend. However, in this dream Mom was lying on a hospital bed in a green nightgown. There were nurses all around the bed and Mom had died. She appeared to be floating up over herself, looking down at her dead body. I looked down at her, too. The nurses rolled the bed out of the room. Then I woke up and I cried out in horror.

"I dreamt my mother died! I dreamt that my mother died!" I screamed over and over. Then I thought, No! That's just your fear. Mom was fine before I left her yesterday."

Since I had been out of town working that day, and the next day being a Sunday, I called the nursing home to speak to Mom and all was well. She sounded happy and I got no indication from any of the nurses that she was not doing fine, or that anything might be wrong. I felt quite relieved, hearing her sweet voice and knowing that she was okay.

I spent all day Monday traveling back to Los Angeles. I got home very late that night, and didn't check my phone, but instead, went straight to bed. The next morning at 8:00 a.m., I called the nursing home to speak with Mom and make arrangements for her to come home that upcoming weekend.

"Didn't you get the message that your mom was taken to the hospital yesterday for pneumonia?" the nurse asked.

"No! What happened to her? I just spoke to her on Sunday!" I gasped.

My heart sank when I heard that news. I realized the message deep within that dream might have been a warning to prepare for something coming. The prospect caused my legs to weaken and I felt faint.

"Could this be the beginning of the end?" I asked myself. My dream flashed in my mind again and again and I felt sick. I fell to my knees and said, "Oh God, please don't let this be."

As I pulled myself together, I was in a daze that felt like a nightmare. I managed to get dressed and drive myself to the hospital. When I got to Mom's room, she looked fine and we were excited to see each other. I hugged her tight and I could see the joy in her eyes.

"How do you feel?" I asked.

She nodded and said, "Okay."

As grateful as I felt to see my mother and that she was doing okay, I still wanted answers. I took the nurse aside and asked what was going on with my mom. She relayed the awful news.

"It seems as though that bacteria came back," she said.

"Oh God, no!" I said. My heart just kept steadily sinking. "Now the bacteria is back? I asked. "How did that bacteria come back? It couldn't be back if they used soap."

I knew that the nursing home was not being careful enough. It made me furious. Not only did Mommy have pneumonia, she had that bacteria again. I went outside for a moment to pull myself together but I couldn't.

I snatched my cell phone and called my husband who was in New York taking care of some business at the time. I told him what was happening with Mom and he tried to console me, but it didn't work. As much as I tried to forget, I kept remembering that disturbing dream, and although I kept pushing it away it remained the only thought in my mind.

I went into the hospital's chapel and prayed, "God, please heal my mother, and help me to handle what I fear is ahead."

As I headed back to Mom's room, I decided not to tell her that the bacterial infection had returned. Why tell her anything bad at this point? I put on a brave face and held on to my faith. I came into her room with a big smile and she smiled back at me.

"Mommy, you're going to be okay. I'm going to be taking you home soon," I said.

In my mind and in my heart I believed I would be taking Mom home as soon as these ailments healed in a few days or weeks. I acted like my usual self, and Mom and I started to talk about all of the things we would do when she came home. We put our music on and I could tell she liked that.

I stayed there with Mom all that day. We talked about going to our favorite Christmas concert together, The Colors of Christmas; something she and I did every year together, and it was only two and a half months away. We talked about some of our friends. She loved when I talked about her teen-age years, like we often did. We talked about her graduation day from junior high school, when her Mom walked into the graduation and every head turned to look at her.

Mom had told me that she was never so proud as to say, "That is my mother," as she was that day when everyone asked, "Who is that?" just like Mother was a movie star.

"Mama was sharp that day and no one could believe how young and beautiful she looked," Mom said.

I talked about Buddy Willis again. I could always get a big smile from her when we talked about that Buddy Willis, and this time was no different. I always knew just what to say to her to brighten her mood, and I enjoyed making her happy. Mom and I were the best of friends.

I remember one time before she had to go to the hospital

with shingles, I was putting stockings on her feet and I said, "Oh Ma, we used to talk about everything."

"I'm still here," she exclaimed.

"Yes Ma, you are still here," I responded with the biggest smile on my face. I will never forget that because it reminded me to always live in the moment, and be grateful for what you still have. Right then I felt so grateful to be talking and laughing with my mom. We were our old selves.

"I have a speech to do tomorrow morning," I said as I gathered my belongings to leave. "Mommy, I will see you tomorrow afternoon, okay?"

"Okay," she answered. Then she said, "We all have to take care of ourselves now. You take care of yourself."

"Mom, you know I will," I said, but I wondered, why is she saying that? While there in the room, I had managed to push my dream completely out of my head. Mom looked great. We talked and she appeared to be very happy.

"Go do your work. I'll be okay," she said.

I did my speech the next day. Before I could get back to the hospital to see Mom that afternoon, I got a call telling me that she had been taken into ICU, and a trach-tube put in her mouth and down her throat. I totally freaked out because now, all of a sudden, it seemed as if she had taken a turn for the worse. As soon as I heard that message on my voicemail, I rushed straight to the hospital. Mom could no longer speak and her arms were tied down at the sides of the bed.

"Why is she tied down?" I asked the staff, trying to maintain my composure.

"She keeps pulling the trach out," a nurse said.

About three days later, Mom was taken out of ICU and put into another room but still on the ICU floor. The doctors said she was coming along just fine. My hopes shot back up. Mom had been in the hospital for about three weeks now. She still couldn't speak because of the trach in her throat. But I would talk to her and I knew she understood everything I said.

On September 27, I had some exciting news for my mother. From the day my book, *Situation 101: Relationships, The Good, The Bad and the Ugly*, came out, she told me that she wanted to see me on "The View." When I received the call from New York that they had scheduled me for a taping on September 28, I rushed to the hospital to share the good news with her.

"Mommy, your dream came true," I said with a big smile on my face as I hurried into her room. "I'm going to be on 'The View!'" My book was being featured on the show thanks to my friend Sherri Shepherd.

Mom's eyes lit up and I could see a slight smile on her face. I knew that news made her happy.

"We made it," I told her. "We made it!"

The next day I flew to New York and taped the show.

The producers scheduled it to air on September 30, on Mom's 80th birthday. That morning I went to the hospital with a dozen balloons with one huge balloon that read, "Mom, I love You So. Happy 80th Birthday." I sat next to her on the bed and said, "Look, Mom. On your birthday your girl is going to be on The View. Everything you wish for me comes true, Mom".

I held her hand and we watched the show together. My appearance was like a birthday present to her. There I was on the television screen with Jimmie "J.J." Walker, talking about *Good Times* and my relationship book. Afterwards, we played music and I knew she enjoyed me being there because when

I said, "Mom, I'm here" she became excited and opened her eyes.

That turned out to be one of the best gifts I could have ever given Mom. I was happy and felt a sense of accomplishment, but fear and anguish had their grip on my heart. I never let Mom know the pain that I was enduring, the pain and fear that became my constant companion.

Since only my children, my husband and I lived in Los Angeles, and most of the family still resided New York, everyone called Mom for her birthday. When my sister Yolanda called from Maryland, I put the phone to Mom's ear.

"Happy Birthday, Mom! I love you," I heard Yolanda say, and Mom knew it was her baby speaking, and she was happy, I could tell.

"Do you remember Mom, when you took care of Olivia as a baby?" Yolanda asked. "Well she is now doing well in dance class."

I saw Mom squint her eyes as if to say yes.

"Mom, Sophia is a real fireball," Yolanda continued, referring to Olivia's baby sister, two years younger than her.

Happiness gleamed in Mom's eyes.

I turned to her. "I'm going to walk down the hall and finish talking to Yolanda."

"I'm so glad you called," I said when I was out of earshot of Mom's room.

"Bern, tell me. How does she look? What do you think?" Yolanda asked.

My eyes welled up with tears and I said, "It feels surreal, Yolanda. Last month I had a dream that Mom died." I paused to regain my composure. "Yolanda, things are happening as if God is letting me know this is the end. It's as if He is preparing me for something. I think this is it, Yolanda," Again, I had to pause because the reality overwhelmed me. "It's funny that on Mommy's birthday 'The View' comes on and I'm on there talking about my book. You know she wanted that to happen for me. It's like she gave me a gift too. Yolanda, I think this is it. And it hurts it really hurts. And I dreamt it, Yolanda."

"Bern, be strong." I could hear the hurt in her voice too.

"Okay, Yo, I will," I replied, and we hung up.

I went back into Mom's room and sat with her for a few more hours and then had to go home to see about Brittany. I promised Mom I would bring Brittany by to visit her for her birthday. While we were gone, my oldest daughter, Dior, came by the hospital and spent time with Mom for her birthday.

The next day I went to see Mom early that afternoon. I noticed the arches on Mommy's feet had dropped, and her feet as well as her hands felt a bit cold. I kept rubbing her hands and telling her she would be okay. I left later that afternoon and Mom appeared to be fine and very comfortable.

On the morning of Sunday, Oct. 2 I woke up early and wanted to see Mom. I got dressed and went over to the hospital. When I got there, Mom was awake.

"Ma, I just wanted to see you. I love you, Ma," I said.

I opened a jar of Shea butter and put it on her hands and then her feet, something I did every single day. As I massaged it into her skin, I noticed Mom looking at the corner of the room, as if she saw something. It was very odd. Then all of a sudden, I smelled a sweet aroma, sweeter and far different than the Shea butter. It smelled like perfume but very strong; stronger than I had ever smelled it before. The same aroma of Mommy's angel surrounded her, only this time it magnified by ten. I knew in my heart what was happening. I knew Mom saw her angels.

I wondered why it was so strong. I believe now that the strong smell simply meant more than one angel was present. I believe that Mom saw her mom, my dad and many other family members.

A nurse came into the room and I stopped her.

"Do you smell something, with a perfumed aroma?" I asked. She looked at me strangely.

"No. Maybe it's that cream you're putting on her feet," she said.

Well, that confirmed for me that mommy saw her angels because the Shea butter that I rubbed on her feet had no smell.

"Oh, Ma! You're looking at your angels," I said.

At that moment I felt as if God told me that Mom would be all right, that she would live. But now I know the angels came to tell us that she was in God's hands. They were helping Mom to say goodbye, as she prepared herself to leave me.

I felt the storm brewing within me that entire week. Every day was painful but when I visited with Mom, I tried to stay upbeat for her. That Wednesday I felt a hurt so deep in my soul that I'll never forget it. I felt panicked and anxious all day. I argued with her doctors to do more for her.

"Your mother is very sick," the doctor said.

"Please stop saying that. Just help her," I scowled. I felt as if I was stuck in a maze, going around in a circle with no way out.

I came home and at about 5:30 p.m., I got a very strange feeling; a strong urge to pray for Mom. I told my daughter Brittany and one of her friends, "Come on. Let's pray for MaMa."

After we prayed, we left and went straight to the hospital. Mom appeared to be okay, and the doctors seemed calm. We stayed with her until eleven o'clock that night.

"I have to speak in the morning for the Alzheimer's Association at 9:00 a.m., so I have to be going, but I'll be back here as soon as the speech is over," I said. "I'm going to be speaking about you."

She gave me a slight smile. I kissed her and said, "I love you, Ma."

We left the hospital and went home. It was such a disturbing day that I hadn't even prepared for my speech. I was not very concerned because I planned to talk about my mother; something I had done many times before. But, I didn't speak that next morning for the Alzheimer's Association. Something much bigger occurred.

9.

The Last Night

After leaving the hospital, I felt drained from the anger caused by the failure of the doctors and nurses to do more to help Mom get better. I called every doctor in the hospital that day and the pain from what they told me practically drove me crazy.

"Your mom is very sick," they repeated over and over again.

"Well if she's sick, get her well," I replied.

I had lived in a state of turmoil ever since my dream a month earlier, and that day I felt absolutely miserable. My body was trapped in a crazy maze full of anguish and pain, and no one could direct me out of it.

I lay on the couch that night, with my daughter Brittany on the other couch. She fell asleep, and soon after, I did too.

Right about 2:00 a.m. the phone rang, waking both of us. I jumped off the couch. Brittany and I looked at each other in horror. She checked the phone's Caller ID.

"Mom that is the hospital, answer it," she said.

I couldn't move and just looked at the phone as it rang and rang and finally went to voicemail.

"Mom, call them back," Brittany said after it stopped ringing.

I knew why they called but I didn't want to talk to them.

I didn't want to face the inevitable bad news. Reluctantly, I listened to the voicemail.

"Please come to the hospital because your mom's vitals are failing," the message said.

"What...is this it? Is my mom dying?" I shrieked

The moment had come. It felt so unreal just like I was frozen in place.

Brittany finally broke the silence. "Come on, Mom. We have to get ourselves together."

Brittany gathered my pants, blouse, my shoes and I slowly got dressed.

She then handed me my purse and keys. "Come on, Mom. MaMa is waiting for us. Now pull yourself together Mom, 'cause you have to drive. I can't drive," Brittany said.

She was sixteen years old but didn't have her license yet. My husband was in New York working so it was just my two daughters and I in Los Angeles with Mom.

On our way to the hospital, Brittany called her older sister and told her to meet us at the hospital. When we arrived, Dior was already there. We went up to ICU and stood at the door to her room.

I felt as if I could hear God tell me, "This is not about you. This is going to happen. Don't make it bad for her, because you don't want her to go into eternity upset."

I knew that God had just given me a blessing and a grace. Before then, I had doubts about what I should do. But now the peace of God was in me and in the room with Mom. God's strength made it possible for me to be strong for my mom.

I walked into the room and looked at Mom lying there so quiet and tranquil. I knew she was waiting for me. "Mom, I'm here, and you're not going to go through this by yourself. I'm going to lay right next to you. If it takes a minute, an hour, a week or a month, I'm going to lay right here with you," I said.

I had the nurse move Mom over, give me a blanket and pillow, and I lay in the bed right next to her. I put my foot over her foot, so that she would know that I was there with her. Mom still had the trach down her throat, so she couldn't speak anymore, but it was as if I could hear what she was thinking. Silence engulfed the room so quiet and so peaceful. No doubt, the presence of God was in there with us.

I could see the clock on the wall. It was about 2:15 a.m. The nurse said she had called the priest to come in to pray for Mom. My daughters were in the waiting room down the hall from Mom's room, resting. While we waited for the priest, it was so peaceful in that room and in my mother's arms I fell asleep.

When I woke up, I saw that it was 4:30 a.m. For a second, I panicked, realizing where I was and that Mom lay next to me. I looked over to see if she was still with me. She was. I could not believe I had fallen asleep.

"The priest is here," a nurse came in and said. "I am going to bring him in."

I rushed down the corridor and got my daughters out of the waiting room. The priest came and said prayers for Mom, then paid her a beautiful compliment.

"Your mom must have been an awesome woman because you are such a very strong woman, and I know she is very proud," he said.

I thanked him. It was God's gift to my mother that His peace and presence was there with her and with us on this last night together. We continued to pray for Mom and when the priest finished, he left.

About a half hour later, I sat at the foot of the bed and the room remained still very quiet and very, very calm. My daughter, Dior, went around to Mom's side of the bed and looked at her.

"Ma...MaMa's eyes look different," she said.

"Show her the picture of Jesus that's next to her," I said.

Dior showed Mom the 8x10-inch picture of Jesus we kept next to her bed. Mom didn't respond. Her eyes appeared to be far away.

"Show her the picture of Mary," I said. She loved the mother of Jesus.

Dior showed her the picture of Mary. "Ma, she's not focusing. It's like she's looking through the picture," Dior said.

I went around to the side of the bed, and looked into my mother's eyes. Her eyes wandered around the room, as if gazing on something amazing.

"Dior, I think she's looking at the real thing," I said. I could see the whites of her eyes starting to turn a little yellow, and then I could see tiny, little red blood vessels appearing.

"Oh, my God! I'm looking into the eyes of death," I whispered. My heart was breaking, and I knew I had to talk to Mommy.

"I love you, Ma. I started and couldn't stop. "I love you, I love you, I love you, I love you, I love you, I love you, I love you, I love you, I love you, I love you, I love you, I love you and I know you love me too. Mama we had fun, we had a good time...but I won't let it end yet."

Then Mommy left.

The nurses called code blue and rushed us out of the room. We went into the waiting room while they tried to bring Mom back.

After what seemed like an eternity, the nurse came back into the waiting room.

"We have a pulse," she said. "We don't know how long it will last and what do you want us to do if we lose her again?

"Resuscitate," I said.

While I talked with the nurse, Brittany called Kyle and he asked to speak with me.

"Bern, let her go," he said. "It's very painful for Mom to keep having to come back. Just let her go, okay," As a pastor I knew his words were inspired by God.

"Okay, I will," I said reluctantly. "You know, the strangest thing happened when I was lying next to Mom," I continued. "Can you believe I fell asleep for two hours lying in Mommy's arms?"

Kyle spoke comforting words to me.

"Bern, you had to fall asleep in Mom's arms because that was God letting Mommy know that you'll be okay. The Comforter had to let Mommy know you'll be okay. Mommy needed to know that so she could go into eternity with the peace she needs in order to rest."

The nurse came in again.

"We lost your mom again," she said. "She's gone. What do you want us to do? Do you want us to try and get her back?"

I shook my head no and nodded with the realization that Mom had moved on.

After the nurse went in and disconnected Mom from the ventilator and the machines they used to monitor her vitals, she came back out and said.

"You can go in now if you want to be with her."

I couldn't go back in right at that moment. I didn't know how she would look.

"I'll go in," Dior said as she first hugged me and disappeared inside the room.

"Ma, I'm going in too," Brittany said, "and see if MaMa looks okay, I'll tell you, so you can come in and see her." Brittany finished and followed her sister into the room.

"Fine," I said.

I stood outside the room anxious for one of my daughters to come back out. I knew I'd be able to tell Mom's condition by the expression on their face.

Brittany came back out first. "Ma, she looks like she's asleep," she said.

That's all the encouragement I needed. I went into the room and Mommy really did look like she had just gone off to sleep. I remembered she had told me that the hearing was the last to go when you die, so I began talking to her.

"Oh Mommy, you look beautiful, and I'm going to fix you so pretty. Okay?"

I looked at her pretty face and her left eye had not completely closed. I put my hand over her eye and said, "Mom, I am closing your eye." I closed it. Then I closed her mouth because it was slightly opened, too. It looked as if there was a tearstain on her cheek.

"Ma, I am going to wash your face for the last time. Okay?" I walked over to the wash basin, got a cloth and washed her face. Then I turned her music on so she could hear the music she loved. God was all around us. The feeling was not sad, but one of understanding.

By this time, my brother had made the arrangements for Mom to go to a funeral home in Los Angeles. The people from the funeral home had arrived and said they had to put her in the black bag to transport her. I said to my daughters, "I can't watch them put my mom in a black body bag."

"Mom, you leave. I'll stay in the room with Mama," Brittany said.

She stayed and Dior and I left.

They took Mom, and we followed them to the funeral home. They embalmed her and got everything arranged for her to be sent back to New York. I went home and got Mom's nightclothes and housecoat so that she would be covered while being prepared for the plane ride home. Then I got all of Mom's clothes ready for her funeral.

The next day Dior and I went to the funeral home to groom Mom. Dior did Mommy's hair. She pressed, rolled and pin-curled it, and then tied it up and it looked beautiful. I did my mom's nails and makeup. Mom looked so natural and beautiful, just as she always did. This was not easy for us to do, but something we had to do for her. No one could press and curl Mom's hair like Dior could, and I knew just how she would like her makeup. I had to be the one to do it.

During all of this I didn't cry. I was at peace and in quiet control, as if I was in a bubble of protection. I knew Mom had transcended from one state of existence to another. Her spirit was the same and right there with me through everything.

I thought of the dream I had a month earlier when she and I both looked down upon her. Mom's strength was with me.

In three days, everything was ready and we left for New York. We arrived a day before Mom's body did in order to complete the final planning and preparation.

When Mom arrived at the funeral home in New York, the female undertaker, who was there to dress her, reassured me that Mom would be beautiful. The next day we went to see how Mom looked, and she did look as beautiful as the woman promised me.

When I touched Mom's arm as she lay there in her baby blue casket and her baby blue St. Johns suit, I felt a plastic suit underneath her clothes. It was not noticeable unless you touched her, but I didn't understand why it was there, so I asked the woman who dressed her.

"Your mom was on a ventilator when she was in the hospital, and the water in her body from being on the ventilator was leaking out. That's why we put a plastic suit on her body before we put her clothes on," the attendant told me.

It was a reasonable explanation. I gave the funeral home my approval for how well they made Mom look. Everything about Mommy was beautiful.

The day of her funeral plans were set and perfect. My mom's service was at my brother's church, but Kyle had a visiting pastor to preside over it because he was too grief-stricken to do it. All five of Mom's children sat in the front pew. We all decided that the funeral should be lively and not sad. A few of my mom's grandchildren came up and spoke about her and then I said a few words.

I strolled up to the podium and stood for a few moments in order to control my emotions. This was not a script like I had for *Good Times*, but straight from my heart, not rehearsed but real time. I began,

"Mom, your call to do your duty for the world is now over. You gave humanity three daughters and two sons. You upheld your honor to be with only one man, a husband who loved and respected you to the highest." I paused as I felt my voice cracking from emotions. "Mom, your call to do your duty to the world is done. You made your mother and your father proud and honored their name. Your mark, your vision, your love for them and your family will live on and will never die.

"Whatever you didn't accomplish no one can ever say it was because you didn't try. I will forever remember the lessons you have taught, the fights you fought for the love of your family. There has never been a mother that mothered better than you. Never a person who was fairer than you. Now Mom, it is your time to be free and let your beautiful soul take to the air.

"We know you will always be here with us in spirit and surround us with your love. We want to thank you Mother for being who you were, thank you Mother for being our mother. Every one of us is proud to be called Eula's children. Enjoy the peace in your sleep Mom, and know that we will do our best to make and keep you proud.

"Our love, forever, will be with you Mommy."

With tears freely flowing down my cheeks, I finished and returned to my seat. Then all five of us got up and gathered around her casket.

"This is where we cover her face with a velvet cloth, and we close the casket," Kyle said.

Still, with tears in my eyes I looked at him. "Is this the last time I will see Mommy?" I asked.

"No. Tomorrow, at the burial, we will open it one last time," he said in a very sympathetic voice. He knew how much I was hurting.

I was fine because I knew this would not be the last time I would see my mom's face. We laid the purple, velvet cloth over her face and closed the casket. The pastor ended the service and Mommy was taken out of the church.

Early the next morning, we were on our way to Veteran's Cemetery where my father was buried. Mommy's casket was in the cathedral, awaiting the last rites. There stood a Catholic priest ready to pray for Mom. I turned to my brother Kyle and asked him when the casket would be opened so I could see Mommy for the last time.

"We're not, Bern," he said.

His words stung me like an electric shot through my body. I felt such hurt and pain because now it was final. I would not see my mother ever again. I lost all the reserve that I had used to that point. I went up to Mommy's casket and I lay on it and cried from the depths of my soul. I realized I had to leave my mom there in the cemetery forever. I didn't want to leave my mother in that lonely place.

"Oh, Momma, Momma, Momma. I love you so much. I don't want to leave you, Momma. I don't want to leave you." I cried and cried.

No one could pull me off Mom's casket so they left me alone for what seemed an hour. Then, my brothers escorted me to the limousine that was waiting for us. The hurt was like none I have ever felt before.

In the limousine my brother explained things to me.

"Bern, I had to tell you that we were going to open it again because we knew if I didn't tell you that, we wouldn't be able to ever close it."

I accepted his explanation because I knew he was right. I would never have let them close her casket as easy as they did in the church, if I'd known that would be my last look upon my mother's pretty face. What really eased my heart was the fact that she would be there buried right on top of Dad. He was twelve-feet under, and as he'd always said, Mom's casket would be buried on top of his. He had been waiting for her. It was time for them to spend eternity together.

Rest now my beloved parents. You both have done well. Your job is complete here. Now rest in eternity together. My love is forever.

EPILOGUE

REMEMBERING MAMA

My daughters had a special bond with their grandmother and were involved in her care. I hope that by sharing their experiences, they are able to help other family members of a caregiver.

"The Last Night" by Brittany Rose

It wasn't an easy transition when my parents told me, at such a young age, that in a few months I would have to share them. I was used to having them to myself all the time being that my sister and I had such a big age gap. And, my parents had the role of parents as well as playmates all my life.

They told me that my grandmother had a disease that caused her not to remember things she was used to remembering and that she needed to live with us for some time. At first I though it was a temporary thing, but as the months passed which later turned into years, I matured and realized my "MaMa" would need me to be a big girl and take care of her more than ever. My selfish ways quickly went away, after Mom and Dad explained to me that not many children have it in them to help their parents to take care of their grandparent the way I had. When they explained this to me it made me want to help out even more, because nothing made me happier in life than to know that my parents were proud of me.

My grandmother's disease progressively got worse, and day-by-day it took over all of our lives. However, instead of being sad about it my family and I embraced every day we had with her, and didn't make her feel that things were as bad as they actually were. We made sure to have more laughter than tears and more hugs than heartaches. Looking back on it, although Alzheimer's is a sad disease, we had much to laugh about.

I remember doing a paper in tenth grade for school one night, and I was looking everywhere for a dictionary in order to find the spelling of one word that I simply couldn't spell. I was so frustrated. I spoke out loud and said, "This is impossible. How do you spell catastrophe?" My grandmother instantly woke up from her nap and started spelling the word perfectly. I was so shocked. It showed me that some things never leave the brain and it made me smile. After spelling the word, she went right back to sleep. It was one of the cutest things ever.

What Alzheimer's taught me was that it's very hard to say goodbye to someone you love and cherish so much. The reason this disease was so difficult was because I had to say goodbye a little more every day, to a phenomenal woman who never deserved this. In 2011, I said my final goodbye to an eighty-year-old queen. Though that night in the hospital was a difficult one, it was very peaceful, and I know my grandmother is looking down smiling at me today.

A Granddaughter's Reflections by Dior Ravél

My relationship with my grandmother was very kind, encouraging and educational. She taught me so much in the short time I would spend with her, being that I lived in Los Angeles and she lived in New York City. I visited her from time to time, and the times I was there were most endearing and adventurous. She was the only grandparent that gave me these feelings.

While in the city she always kept me very close to her, especially when I moved to the city for a semester of school. It was like we were glued at the hip. From the time I would leave for school in the morning and take the train, then the bus and then walk almost ten blocks, she was only a few steps away. She said, "I guess because you're almost a senior in high school, I won't walk right beside you. I'll give you some freedom, and I'll walk on the opposite side of the street." She would have it no other way. New York is a lot to take in, and when you move from one coast to the other it can be overwhelming. MaMa gave me her courage to conquer the city one step at a time. Living with her, I was able to see how strong and fearless she was about her life there; she truly was a New Yorker with all the bells and whistles.

Many years later my grandmother became ill, and I remember it like it was yesterday. My mother walked in my room and said in a very serious but troubling manner, "Mama is coming to live with us. She can't do it alone anymore." I was like, "She can't do it anymore? How is that, because she was always so strong and independent?" But that was the end of it; nobody questioned the decision again. We knew what we had to do.

By the time my grandmother moved in, she was clearly well into the first stages of the Alzheimer's disease. During the first stages of the disease, it was unnoticeable how far along my grandmother was, but it was also extremely scary watching this invisible monster grow around us. There were many days and nights that I had to be told to remember that my loving MaMa is no longer the same person. Every day was a different day; she would do strange and odd things that would make us all nervous. The progression of the disease was so fast that as a family, we had to adapt a new way of living and not run away from what we didn't know. We could only embrace this invisible monster that was growing inside our dear MaMa. There is no counseling or class that can prepare you for losing a family member like this. It's truly a love walk that the person and the family must take together.

Tears filled my mother's eyes when she would have to go on tour without her mother, knowing it was for the best. My grandmother was always in the best care, but the pain of her condition always got the best of all of us.

One of the most memorable moments I shared with my grandmother was one weekend when she came to hang out with me, and go with me and run errands for the day. At this time, she was at the stage where she could still walk around and enjoy the outside, without being too worried about things. I truly feel like it was our special day together. We had a moment where she and I connected, and I saw a glimpse of her as a young girl. The disease opened her mind and took her back to a place where she had to be mid-twenties or so. She started to tell me stories of herself, and although the stories blended together, it was such a pleasure to hear her speak of joyous memories. I was so delighted to have heard this come from her; I never knew my grandmother this way. She continued to talk the whole day. She was laughing, smiling and she told me things about her being a painter and dancer. We laughed, and she was non-stop jokes the whole time. Who knew how a nasty little disease could bond two people together in such a way?

Above: Mom at age 21
Below: Me at the pageant where I was discovered.

Acting headshots

Above: Esther and I on the set of *Good Times*.
Below: Esther backstage at a play I produced.

Above: Mom and I at her 76th birthday dinner.
Below: Celebrating Mom's 76th birthday at Lawry's
in Beverly Hills.

Above: Mom visiting me in Los Angeles
Below: Mom receiving the Mom Acheivement
Award

Above: Dancing with my father
Below: Mom before Alzheimer's

Above: Mom and Dad having fun on an exercise
bike
Below: Mom and Dad

Above: Mom on Easter Sunday at my brother Kyle's church
Below: Mom at my brother Kyle's church.

Above: My daughter Dior
Below: My daughter Brittany Rose

QUOTES FROM EULA AND GREG'S BOOK OF LIFE

With education behind you and determination within you, there is no place in the world you cannot go.

Keep your nose clean!

Don't take wooden nickels!

What's for you is for you, and no one can take it from you.

You go there and learn as much as you can, and ignore those people.

You have to show people what you can do. How else will they know that you have talent?

Let people see how good you are.

Don't be shy because those people are just people, just like you, that's all they are.

No one is better than you, and you have just as much talent as they have, no matter what they think of you.

Keep focused, and get on with the business of learning.

No one can stop you if you are determined to reach a goal.

Help somebody.

Just go in there and do your thing.

Everybody has different talents.

Don't let fear stop you from walking into your destiny. (Mom and Dad had great quotes, but this quote is mine!)

Greg and Eula's Babies

Children	Grandchildren	Great Grandchildren
Bernadette	Dior Ravél Brittany Rose Cole Marina (adopted)	Leto MaNon Ah'Mia
Gregory Kyle	Jacques Asia Paris Cairo Sienna	Ella and Nina
Talbert Kethrell	Tyson (Lil Trell) Sharrell Amber Ashley Alexys Zari Prince Aubrei	Brooklyn and Elle
Deborah	Kirsten Zeke Joshua	Todd and Kiko
Yolanda	Olivia Sophia	

THE CAREGIVER'S RESOURCE GUIDE

WHAT IS ALZHEIMER'S?

Alzheimer's disease, also known as AD or simply Alzheimer's, was discovered by Alois Alzheimer, a German psychiatrist, who first described this condition in 1906. He was one of the first to link the symptoms of the disease to microscopic changes in the brain. In one of his patients he found profound memory loss and other deteriorating psychological changes. He studied her brain through autopsy, and it was there that he saw dramatic shrinkage and abnormal deposits in and around brain nerve cells.

Alzheimer's is a chronic neurodegenerative disease that usually starts slowly and gets worse over time. It slowly steals the minds of its victims, leading to memory loss, confusion, impaired judgment, personality changes, disorientation and the inability to communicate.

Since its discovery, there is still little known about its causes and there is still no known cure.

WHAT IS DEMENTIA

Dementia is a general term for loss of memory severe enough to interfere with daily life. Dementia is caused by a variety of diseases and medical or psychological conditions, but Alzheimer's is the most common type of dementia. Alzheimer's dementia accounts for an estimated 60 to 80 percent of all dementia cases.

Dementia is characterized by a decline in memory, language, problem-solving and other cognitive skills that affects a person's ability to perform everyday activities. This decline occurs because nerve cells (neurons) in parts of the brain involved in cognitive function have been damaged and no longer function normally. In Alzheimer's disease, neuronal damage eventually affects parts of the brain that enable a person to carry out basic bodily functions such as walking and swallowing.

WHO WILL GET ALZHEIMER'S?

This disease has no color line, which means people of all nationalities get it and are living with the disease. But African Americans get this disease twice-to-three-times as much as other races. What we are learning is that high blood pressure and cholesterol are contributing factors of Alzheimer's. Another risk factor is family history. Research has shown that those who have a parent, brother or sister with Alzheimer's are more likely to develop the disease than individuals who do not. The risk increases if more than one family member has the illness.

Scientists have identified three genes that guarantee individuals will develop Alzheimer's, but only a very small percentage of people with Alzheimer's (about 1 percent) carry these genes. Therefore there may be more factors out there causing Alzheimer's besides the ones I have already mentioned. The three genes are APOE -e4, APOE -e2 and APOE-e3. The complex part of this disease is that although individuals may carry these genes and are more likely to develop Alzheimer's, there is still no guarantee that they will develop the disease. With this information, many people may not want to get tested or volunteer for clinical trials, but although you may carry these genes, there is no need to panic because you may still never get the disease. This is why this disease is so hard to track down. Experts believe the vast majority of Alzheimer's cases are caused by a complex combination of genetic andnon-genetic influences.

We must help pinpoint its origin, and that's why it is so very important that we participate in clinical trials. African-Americans must do so in order to find out why they are affected twice to three times as much as any other group of people. And it will take African-Americans to participate in the clinical trials to help find the answer for African-Americans.

ALZHEIMER'S SYMPTOMS

Alzheimer's disease symptoms vary among individuals. The most common initial symptom is a difficulty to remember new information that gradually worsens. This memory decline occurs because the first neurons to malfunction and die in the brain are usually neurons in brain regions involved in forming new memories rather than the areas that control long-term memory.

The symptoms of Alzheimer's disease gradually worsen over a number of years. As neurons in other parts of the brain malfunction and die, individuals experience other symptoms of the disease. These include memory loss that disrupts daily life, challenges in planning or solving problems, and trouble completing familiar tasks at home, at work or at leisure. Other symptoms range from a general sense of confusion that can't be pinpointed, confusion with time or place, and problems understanding pictures and visual images as well as difficulty with perspective, distance and spatial relationships.

As the disease progresses, individuals lose their ability to carry on a conversation and respond to their environment or they may have problems with words in speaking or writing. Those with Alzheimer's may also suffer from changes in mood and personality. They may start to avoid friends, family or may withdraw from social situations. Or they may seem sad, distant, irritable, unusually angry or depressed.

How rapidly or slowly the symptoms advance from mild to severe differs from person to person. But with all cases, as the brain degenerates and the disease progresses, the cognitive and functional abilities of the person with Alzheimer's will decline. Daily activities such as bathing, dressing, eating and using the bathroom will require assistance. People may also start to not recognize relatives and loved ones, a particularly painful symptom for the loved ones who are no longer recognized.

In the final stages of the disease patients usually become bedbound and reliant on around- the-clock care. They cannot walk or move around the way they used to. They become more susceptible to infections including pneumonia, which is often a contributing factor to the death of people with Alzheimer's disease.

ALZHEIMER'S DETECTION AND SURVIVAL

Early detection and diagnosis is the best way to handle this disease. It allows for early use of available treatments that may provide some relief of symptoms and help those diagnosed maintain their independence longer. Early diagnosis will give the person diagnosed the opportunity to make important legal and financial decisions. It will also allow the patient to be a part of their care plans while they are still capable, allowing them to make their preferences known to their families. Early detection also allows an individual the opportunity to participate in clinical trials.

Those with the disease can live an average of 8 years after their symptoms become noticeable to others. Survival can range from four to 20 years depending on age and other health conditions. I believe with education and awareness and participation in clinical trials, we will get closer to its cause and hopefully find the cure to end this devastating disease known to us as Alzheimer's.

TEN WARNING SIGNS OF ALZHEIMER'S

Knowing the 10 signs of Alzheimer's will help with early detection.

1. **Memory loss that disrupts daily life.** In the early stages of Alzheimer's, one forgets recently learned information. Other signs are forgetting important dates or events, asking for the same information over and over and increasingly needing to rely on memory aids. For example, reminder notes or electronic devices or family members for things they used to handle on their own. The difference from age-related change is sometimes one will forget names or appointments, but will remember them later.

2. **Challenges in planning or solving problems.** Some people may experience changes in their ability to develop and follow a plan or work with numbers. They may have trouble following a familiar recipe or keeping track of monthly bills. They may have difficulty concentrating and take much longer to do things than they did before. The difference from age-related change is making occasional errors when balancing a checkbook.

3. **Difficulty completing familiar tasks at home, at work or at leisure.** People with Alzheimer's often find it hard to complete daily tasks. Sometimes, people may have trouble driving to a familiar location, managing a budget at work or remembering the rules of a favorite game. The difference from age-related change is, occasionally needing help to use the settings on a microwave or to record a television show.

4. **Confusion with time or place.** People with Alzheimer's can lose track of dates, seasons and the passage of time. They may have trouble understanding something if it is not happening immediately. Sometimes they may forget where they are or how they got there. The difference from age-related change is getting confused about the day of the week but we figuring it out later.

5. **Trouble understanding visual images or how objects fit together in relation to space.** For some people having visual problems is a sign of Alzheimer's. They may have difficulty reading judging the distance and determining color or contrast, which may cause problems with driving. The difference from age-related change is vision changes related to cataracts.

6. **New problems with words in speaking or writing.** People with Alzheimer's may have trouble following or joining a conversation. And they may stop in the middle of a conversation and have no idea how to continue or they may repeat themselves. They may struggle with vocabulary, have problems finding the right word or call things by the wrong name. For example they may call a "watch" a "hand-clock." The difference from age-related change is sometimes having trouble finding the right word.

7. **Misplacing things and losing the ability to retrace steps.** A person with Alzheimer's disease may put things in unusual places. They may lose things and be unable to go back over the steps to find them again. Sometimes, they may accuse others of stealing. This may occur more frequently over time. The difference from age-related change is misplacing things from time to time and retracing steps to find them.

8. **Decreased or poor judgment.** People with Alzheimer's may experience changes in judgment or decision making. For example, they may use poor judgment when dealing with money, giving large amounts to telemarketers. They may pay less attention to grooming or keeping themselves clean. The difference from age-related change is making a bad decision once in a while.

9. **Withdrawal from work or social activities.** A person with Alzheimer's may start to remove themselves from hobbies, social activities, work projects and sports. They may have trouble keeping up with their favorite sports team or remembering how to complete a favorite hobby. They may also avoid being social because of the changes they have experienced. The difference from age-related change is sometimes feeling weary of work, family and social obligation.

10. **Changes in mood and personality.** The mood and personality of people with Alzheimer's can change. They can become confused, suspicious, depressed, fearful or anxious. They may be easily upset at home, at work, with friends or in places where they are out of their comfort zone. The difference from age-related change is developing very specific ways of doing things and becoming irritable when a routine is disrupted.

FOLLOWING A DIAGNOSIS

The diagnosis of Alzheimer's can be a devastating blow to the family being affected. There's anger, confusion, fear, grief and so many emotions to deal with at once. The best and first thing one can do is to arm themselves with as much information as possible. That seems simple enough, but where do you turn? I've compiled this list to help you get the information you need to deal with this disease.

HOW TO LEARN MORE ABOUT AD

Talk with a doctor or other health care provider about AD. Make a list of any and all questions that you have and don't be afraid to ask them again and again until you have clarity. Sometimes medical jargon can be confusing, but there is no reason that a qualified medical professional won't explain things to you in terms that are easier for you to understand. Then, ask them to refer you to someone who specializes in Alzheimer's disease.

Your doctor or Alzheimer's specialist can lead you to good sources of information. After all, this is their area of expertise so don't hesitate to tap into their knowledge.

Check out books, CD's, DVD's, or videos on AD from the library. Ask the librarian for help if you aren't comfortable navigating through the stacks of books alone. They are more than happy to help you, and because they get so many people who may be researching the same subjects, they can be a very helpful source of information.

Attend educational programs and workshops on AD. This will help keep your personal knowledge base up to date and you may meet others who will be able to advise or support you and your family.

Visit websites on Alzheimer's Disease such as:

www.alzheimers.gov,

www.nia.nih.gov/alzheimers, or

www.alz.org

for the latest in Alzheimer's information. Use search engines to find more information from newspapers, magazines, blogs and medical journals.

Talk about AD with friends and family to get advice and support. You never know who has dealt with this disease and hasn't shared it with you or who can help lift your spirits when you are down.

It is important for you to try and find a support group for caregivers.

You may want to find a group in which the caregivers are taking care of someone who is in the same stage of AD as the person you are caring for. You may also be able to find an Internet-based support group. This is helpful for some caregivers, because it means they don't have to leave home to be a part of the group. The Alzheimer's Association (*www.alz.org*) may be able to help you find support groups as well.

WHO IS AFFECTED BY ALZHEIMER'S?

According to the World Health Organization, in 2010 there were between 21 and 35 million people worldwide with AD. That number is projected to increase to 75 million by 2030 and 135 million by 2050.

According to the Alzheimer's Association. An estimated 5.3 million Americans of all ages have Alzheimer's disease in 2015, and by 2050, as the U.S. population ages, this number could increase to nearly 14 million.

Alzheimer's is not a normal part of aging, although the greatest known risk is age. And Alzheimer's is not a disease that is exclusive to the elderly. While it is a fact that the majority of people with Alzheimer's are 65 and older, approximately 200,000 individuals are under age 65 (younger-onset Alzheimer's).

Almost two-thirds of Americans with Alzheimer's are women. Of the 5.1 million people age 65 and older with Alzheimer's in the United States, 3.2 million are women and 1.9 million are men.

In United States, older African-Americans and Hispanics are more likely than older whites to have Alzheimer's disease and other dementias.

THE SILENT POPULATION AFFECTED BY ALZHEIMER'S

There is also another population that is affected by Alzheimer's—the caregiver. While not afflicted by physical symptoms, the emotional impact for those who care for loved ones who suffer with Alzheimer's disease and dementia is enormous.

In 2014, friends and family of people with Alzheimer's and other dementias provided an estimated 17.9 billion hours of unpaid care, a contribution that is valued at an estimated $217.7 billion. It is estimated that 250,000 children and young adults between ages 8 and 18 provide help to someone with Alzheimer's disease or another dementia.

SOME ADDITIONAL FACTS ABOUT CAREGIVERS:

Approximately two-thirds of caregivers are women and 34 percent are age 65 or older.

Forty-one percent of caregivers have a household income of $50,000 or less.

Over half of primary caregivers of people with dementia take care of their parents.

Alzheimer's takes a devastating toll on caregivers. Nearly 60 percent of Alzheimer's and dementia caregivers rate the emotional stress of caregiving as high or very high; about 40 percent suffer from depression. Due to the physical and emotional toll of caregiving, Alzheimer's and dementia caregivers had $9.7 billion in additional health care costs of their own in 2014.

TO TELL OR NOT TO TELL

Let us be real about this point, we don't want others to see our loved one in an unfavorable light. There seems to be a reluctance to reveal a diagnosis of Alzheimer's or any other form of dementia to others. I can understand this reluctance because there is a need to protect those whom we love. If, for example, my husband is becoming quick-tempered and suspicious because of the damage to the brain from Alzheimer's disease, I do not want my close neighbor to see this behavior. I am embarrassed for him. This feeling is understandable. But, there can be an advantage to informing family members and close friends about what is happening to our loved one.

Here are important reasons why:

- Educating family and friends about the disease may help them feel more comfortable around the person with the disease. Personality and mood changes will be easier to handle if others understand why they are happening. Educating others to understand that it is the disease and not the person who is causing the changes is also helpful.
- As a caregiver you have opened up to others who can now share your feelings. No one should face this disease alone.
- As we share with others and educate what Alzheimer's is we de-stigmatize the disease.
- The earlier the detection, the more beneficial some of the medications can be.
- Alzheimer's is a medical condition, not a psychological/ emotional disorder or a contagious virus.
- Explaining the responsibility of caregiving and how it affects your life will help others have a better sense of how they can help you.
- If there are children and teenagers in the family it is good to talk with them because they have their concerns too. Sometimes if they have a grandparent with Alzheimer's they may worry that

maybe their parent will get it at some point in time.

Young children are often able to relate to a person who has limited verbal ability. Teenagers and young adults feel valued if they are offered an opportunity to spend time with the person or share some of your responsibilities.

COMMUNICATING AS A CAREGIVER

Some people think that because a person has Alzheimer's that they are crazy or at worst, a non-person. Caregivers are charged with the task that they must remember that those who suffer from the disease are adults who have altered behaviors due to a brain injury. They must be treated with respect and consideration. They should be treated like they are valuable people who are wanted.

What I have learned from my mother is that the most valuable part of an Alzheimer's patient is still in there, you just have to see and hear them now with a deeper way of looking and hearing. It's as if one has to learn a new language. The person with Alzheimer's still communicates, but it is mostly through non-verbal actions such as facial expressions or quiet body language.

Being around the person with AD, you will learn what they like or dislike. Watch them closely and you will see that you will understand what they want and need more clearly. Just take your time and have patience with them. The person with AD can still see and can still hear and most of all they can still feel. So when people talk about them like they are an object in the room, it's rude and hurtful because they hear what you are saying about them. Please be considerate of their feelings just as you would anyone else. They may not be able to express in words or complete sentences what they may want to do or say, but their feelings are still inside. Sometimes they become extra sensitive, and they can sense when someone does not want to deal with them. This will be expressed by them becoming stubborn or they may ignore anything you are trying to get them to do.

We were very fortunate with my mom because she still could communicate with me, my husband and both my daughters. I believe that was because we were with her every day, and we communicated with her constantly. We learned her new language. We knew what she meant when she did certain things and what she was conveying.

Her reactions and facial movements meant certain things we all came to recognize and know.

This disease affects each person who has it differently but it is up to the caregiver to remain positive no matter what and find the silver lining in this dark cloud of a disease.

POSITIVE ASPECTS OF CAREGIVING

Caring for someone you love like a parent can be emotionally fulfilling.

- Being needed by a loved one makes one feel valuable.
- Caregiving often gives feelings of accomplishment.
- You will find personal strength and courage previously unknown.
- Families can become closer.
- Patience, forgiveness and humor are character builders.
- You will learn to value the present.
- Hallmarks of Good Caregiving
- By understanding these hallmarks, you will be an excellent caregiver.
- Work out a plan of your own for survival.
- There is no one right way, just your way.
- Although our loved one may not know who we are, we know who they are.
- The patient has no control over what is happening to him or her.
- There is no reasoning with dementia patients.
- There are solutions to every workable problem.
- Persons with Alzheimer's disease can still learn.
- There is still creativity in the Alzheimer's patient.
- The person with Alzheimer's disease is a human being; we must not forget that.
- Find the hidden treasures in Alzheimer's disease. They really are there.

CAREGIVER ACTIVITIES

Here are some of the things I did with my mother to keep her active and alert that might work with your loved one.

- We listened to music. The song that she loved to hear was Michael McDonald's "Ain't No Mountain High Enough."
- I would read articles off of the internet to her that I thought would interest her or hold her attention.
- We looked at family photos. This helped our family maintain their connection with my mother.
- We remained creative. We would color pictures from our coloring books and went to a watercolor class.
- Babies and the elderly often have a special connection. I invited my neighbors who had small babies to come over and visit with us when ever they could.
- Mom and I would fold clothes, she enjoyed that.
- We sorted playing cards by their color.
- We put simple puzzles together.
- We separated coins and put them into jars.
- Mom used to like to cut up paper for scratch paper.
- We would dance together.
- I would give Mom manicures and take care of her appearance. Just because someone has Alzheimer's doesn't mean they shouldn't look their best. I really do believe this did a lot for my mother's outlook.
- We popped popcorn. The sound of the popping kernels held her attention and when the popcorn was ready we had a delicious and nutritious snack to eat.
- We would look at pictures in the magazines.
- I would read stories out of the Bible. One of her favorite stories was the Book of Esther. She loved that story.

SEVEN STEPS TO BEING A HEALTHY CAREGIVER

Here are seven simple steps you can take to ensure that you are a healthy caregiver:

- See your doctor on a regular basis.
- Get screened for stress and depression, and follow your doctor's advice after a diagnosis of acute stress, anxiety or depression.
- Get plenty of rest. You can't take care of others if you're exhausted.
- Exercise regularly. Exercise keeps the body healthy and clears the mind. Plus, exercise releases endorphins, the chemicals in your body that make you feel happy.
- Eat well-balanced meals. Proper nutrition starts from the inside out. Making sure that you eat healthy will make all the difference in the world with your attitude and energy-levels.
- Accept help from others. No one can make it on their own. Help from others will prevent you from becoming burned-out.
- Call the Alzheimer's Association. They are more than happy to assist you in finding the help that you need.

TEN WAYS TO BE A HEALTHY CAREGIVER

1. **Find time for yourself.** Take advantage of respite care so you can spend time doing something you enjoy. Respite care provides caregivers a temporary rest from caregiving, while the person with Alzheimer's continues to receive care in a safe environment.

2. **Be an informed caregiver.** As the person with dementia shows new behaviors and personality changes, look for ways to respond and cope.

3. **Find support.** Seek support from family, friends, social service agencies and your faith community.

4. **Take care of yourself.** Watch your diet, exercise and get plenty of rest. Also, be sure to visit your doctor to get regular checkups. Maintaining your own health will make you a better caregiver. Ask yourself these questions:

   a.) Do you let others help you? Trying to handle everything by yourself can lead to burnout, depression and resentment.

   b.) Do you talk to others about your feelings? You may think that no one understands. But holding in your feelings will only make you feel isolated and neglected. It's OK to open up.

   c.) Do you see your doctor? Are you overeating? Unable to sleep? Always feeling tired? Not keeping up with routine health care appointments? Take these signs seriously. See a doctor before you experience a health crisis.

5. **Manage your level of stress.** Consider how stress affects your body (stomachaches, high blood pressure) and your emotions (overeating, irritability). Find ways to relax. Check in with your doctor.

6. **Accept changes.** Eventually the person with dementia will need more and more intensive kinds of care. Find out about the options now so you are ready for the changes as they occur.

7. **Plan for the future now.** See an experienced attorney to get legal and financial plans in place. Involve the person with dementia if you can. You may need help in assessing your needs and to create a customized action plan.

8. **Be realistic.** The care you give does make a difference, but many behaviors can't be controlled. Grieve the losses. Focus on positive times as they arise and enjoy good memories.

9. **Do your best.** It's normal to lose patience or feel like your care may fall short sometimes. You're doing the best you can, and the person with dementia feels that you care.

10. **Find Support.** Seek support from family, friends, social service agencies and faith community.

COMMON NEGATIVE FEELINGS EXPERIENCED BY CAREGIVER'S FAMILIES

ANGER...

At the family member with Alzheimer's disease.

At themselves, the caregivers.

At other family members and friends. At health care professionals.

At God.

DENIAL...

Of the disease itself.

Of the need for assistance.

DEPRESSION...

Over the lost relationship with the Alzheimer's person. Over the loss of family continuity.

FEAR...

Of the genetic consequences.

Of the future.

INDECISION...

About financial and legal issues.

About medical care.

About living arrangements.

SELF-PITY...

Over the unfair circumstances in life.

SHAME AND EMBARRASSMENT...

Over the challenging behaviors exhibited by the Alzheimer's patient.

GUILT...

Over past experiences that may have caused the person's condition.

Over the caregiver's own ability to still enjoy life. Over anger with other family members because they live far away, criticize or prefer to remain uninvolved in caregiving.

Over negative feelings and/or problems experienced with the Alzheimer's patient.

Over the ability or inability to provide adequate care.

10 SIGNS OF CAREGIVER STRESS

Checklist

1. Denial about the disease and its effect on the person who has been diagnosed. (*I know Mama is going to get better*)

2. Anger about your loved one having Alzheimer's and that there is no cure or that people just don't understand. (*People just don't understand how hard it is. I'm so angry I could scream!*)

3. Social withdrawal from friends and activities that used to make you feel good. (*I don't feel like getting together with the neighbors anymore.*)

4. Anxiety about the future and facing another day. (*What happens when he/she needs more care than I can provide?*)

5. Depression that breaks your spirit and makes you lose your ability to cope with daily life. (*I just can't take it anymore.*)

6. Exhaustion that makes it nearly impossible to complete the every day tasks that need to get done. (*I'm too tired to cook dinner/bathe/eat, etc.*)

7. Sleeplessness caused by a never-ending list of concerns. (*What if she wanders out of the house or falls and hurts herself?*)

8. Irritability that leads to moodiness and triggers negative responses and reactions. (*Leave me alone!*)

9. Lack of concentration that makes it difficult to do familiar tasks. (*I was so busy, I forgot my appointment*).

10. Health problems that begin to take their toll, both mentally and physically. (*I can't remember the last time I felt good/was happy.*)

TWENTY COPING STRATEGIES FOR CAREGIVERS

Sometimes it is hard for caregivers to cope with the stress and pressure they face. These tips will definitely help you.

1. Keep your identity separate from the patient's identity. Although this can be a hard thing to do, I have learned that it is a must if we are to be our best selves while being a caregiver.

2. Always do things from your center, not the patient's center. This means doing things from your best point of view. Things that will be best for you as well as the loved one you are caring for.

3. Tap into your inner strength and resources. Sometimes under the pressure of caregiving and its challenges, we forget that we have an inner strength and resources that we can count on.

4. Acknowledge all feelings both positive and negative. But reinforce the positive ones because having a positive attitude can get you through the day.

5. Be responsible and take control. Although caregiving can be overwhelming at times we must remember as a caregiver we must show confidence and strength, and that means being responsible for our decisions and taking control of situations at hand.

6. Get information and get help to make caregiving easier. I know that having as much information as you can get as a caregiver will help you make better decisions.

7. Work out your own plan for surviving. Since every life is different we need to work out plans that work for our life as the caregiver.

8. Accept what cannot be changed. We must not let the challenges that we will face as a caregiver destroy our lives but instead we must learn to accept them and truly make the best of what things are and not feel hurt or guilty for what we cannot change.

9. Eliminate words such as "blame" and "excuse" from your vocabulary. Everyone handles life's devastations differently, therefore we must not blame others because they don't handle situations like we would. We must also do the best we can when we can and not use excuses to get out of doing what we know we should.

10. Don't make promises about the future because with diseases such as this there is no future we can rely on. We are living a day to day existence.

11. Think about the worst possible events in your future. This is something we never want to think about but we must. If you understand the worst and consider what you will do in the worst of times, you can be prepared and not overwhelmed.

12. Use respite care regularly for extended blocks of time. There will be times when you must get away from the situation. This is for your sanity, and don't think it's because you are bailing out.

13. Emotional detachment is what you must develop from your caregiving tasks. There will be times when you just have to step back from the situation and rest. Hopefully there will be friends and family members who will understand what you need as a caregiver, and support you in these times with love and understanding.

14. Train yourself to be pro-active to things. If you do this then you will be prepared as much as you can be for the unexpected.

15. Enjoy humor because it assists the immune system. During these times find humor in things. Go to comedy shows, watch comedy on television. These things although are small will help you get through the hard times of reality.

16. Make sure you have a support system that works for you. Surround yourself with people who want to help you feel better about your situation.

17. Be flexible, willing to learn, to adapt, to change. The easier you make your life, the easier it will be to be flexible.

18. "Retrain" your brain with positive reinforcement. The more you are surrounded by positive things the more your brain will become positive. Examples: music, radio, television, people, environment.

19. Do exercises for both the body and soul. Take the time to pay attention to your mind and your body. Simple stretching and visualizing beautiful things every day can do wonders when you are a caregiver.

20. Look for the small joys; they do big wonders. Enjoy buying a scented candle, or a single rose. Buy a different color every few days. It has a way of making you smile throughout a rough day.

TEN WAYS TO HELP A FAMILY LIVING WITH ALZHEIMER'S

1. **Education**

   Educate yourself about Alzheimer's disease. Learn about it and how to respond.

2. **Stay in touch.**

   A card, a call to or a visit means of lot and shows you care.

3. **Be patient.**

   Adjusting to an Alzheimer's diagnosis is an ongoing process and each person reacts differently.

4. **Offer a shoulder to lean on.**

   The diagnosis can create stress for the entire family. Simply offering your support and friendship is helpful.

5. **Engage the person with dementia in conversation.**

   It's important to involve the person in conversation even when his or her ability to participate becomes more limited.

6. **Offer assistance**

   Help the family tackle its to-do list. Prepare a meal, run an errand or provide a ride.

7. **Engage family members in activities.**

   Invite them to go on a walk or participate in other activities.

8. **Offer family members a reprieve.**

   To spend time with the person with dementia so family members can go out alone or visit with friends.

9. **Be flexible.**

   Don't get frustrated if your offer for support is not accepted immediately. The family may need time to assess its needs.

10. **Get involved.**

    Show your support by becoming an advocate or participating in activities to end Alzheimer's.

ALZHEIMER'S INFORMATION GUIDE

This information will detail for you what to expect if *you* are diagnosed with Alzheimer's. It will also help those who are caring for someone with Alzheimer's. Arming yourself with this knowledge will result in a deeper understanding of the symptoms and stages of the disease.

WHAT TO DO IF YOU ARE DIAGNOSED WITH ALZHEIMER'S

There are several things you should be aware of as well as action steps you should follow if you are diagnosed with Alzheimer's. Understand that:

- The changes you are experiencing are because of the disease.
- You will have good days and bad days.
- The disease affects each person differently, and symptoms will vary.
- Trying different ideas will help you find comfortable ways to cope.
- Some suggestions may work for you, others may not.
- You are not alone. An estimated 5 million Americans have Alzheimer's.
- People who understand what you are going through can help you and your family.
- You will have questions following your diagnosis such as:
- What can I do?
- Is what I'm feeling normal?
- How else can I take care of myself?
- What if I live on my own?
- What about the future?
- What can I do to cope with my memory loss?

SOME COMMON FRUSTRATIONS AFTER BEING DIAGNOSED WITH ALZHEIMER'S INCLUDE:

- You may clearly remember things that happened long ago, but recent events can be quickly forgotten.
- You may have trouble keeping track of time, people and places. You may forget appointments or people's names.
- It might be very frustrating trying to remember where you put things.
-

COPING WITH MEMORY LOSS

- These are suggestions for coping with memory loss:
- Keep a notebook of important telephone numbers and addresses, including emergency numbers and your own contact information, with you at all times.
- Write a list of people's names and their rela-tionships to you. Make several copies of this list and place it in your wallet or purse and post it on a wall, bulletin board, or refrigerator. It's also a good idea to give the list to your caregiver if you have one, or a family member or friend.
- Keep a "to-do" list of appointments.
- Print a map showing where your home is. Attach a picture of your home to the map. Make several copies of these documents and place them in your purse or wallet and post them on a bulletin board, wall or refrigerator.
- Keep a journal. Write down thoughts or ideas you want to hold on to.
- Label cupboards and drawers with words or pictures that describe their contents, such as dishes and silverware, or sweaters and socks.
- Get an easy-to-read, digital clock that displays the time and date, and keep it in a prominent place.
- Post phone numbers in large print next to the telephone. Include emergency numbers and a description of where you live.
- Have a dependable friend call you to remind you about meal times, appointments and when to take your medication.
- Keep a set of photos of people you see regularly; label the photos with names and what each does.
- Keep track of the date by marking off each day on a calendar.
- Use pillboxes to help you organize your medication. Pillboxes with sections for times of day, like morning and evening, can help remind you when you should take your pills. There are also pill containers that have alarms to remind you of dosage times.

FINDING YOUR WAY

Sometimes, things that were once familiar to you may now seem unfamiliar. A favorite place may not look the same. Or you might get lost. Here are some suggestions for finding your way:

- Take someone with you when you go out.
- Don't be afraid to ask for help.
- Explain to others that you have a memory problem and need assistance.

COMPLETING DAILY TASKS

You may find familiar activities become more difficult. For example, you may have trouble balancing a checkbook, cleaning and doing housework, following a recipe or doing simple household repairs. Here are some suggestions for completing daily tasks:

- Give yourself a lot of time, and don't let others rush you. Explain to people who might hurry you that you need extra time and ask them to be patient.
- Take a break if something is too difficult or you find yourself becoming frustrated.
- Ask for help if you need it. There's no shame in asking for assistance.
- Arrange for others to help you with difficult tasks in advance.
- Try to maintain a daily routine. Write your routine on paper, cards, or make a chart with pictures and try to follow it.
- As time goes on, certain things may become too difficult for you to do at all. This is because of the disease. Do the best you can, and accept help when
- it's available.

TALKING TO OTHERS

You may have difficulty understanding what others are saying or you may have trouble finding the right words to express your thoughts, but there are ways you can make communication easier. Some suggestions for talking to others include:

- Take your time to think about what you are saying, and take your time when speaking.
- Tell people you are talking to that you have difficulty with communicating and remembering.
- Consider sharing your diagnosis. It can be helpful for family and friends to understand your condition.
- Ask the person you're talking to repeat a statement if you did not understand what was said.
- Find a quiet place to talk if loud noises or crowds bother you.

DEALING WITH THE EMOTIONS OF ALZHEIMER'S

Living with the changes caused by Alzheimer's disease can bring about many unfamiliar emotions. These feelings are a natural response to the disease.

It's important to share these reactions with others. Tell someone with whom you are comfortable how you feel, or consider joining a support group.

You may feel like you worry more than usual. It's important that you share your concerns with your family and friends. You may worry about what's going to happen to you in the future, or you may wonder how quickly the disease will progress. Because Alzheimer's affects everyone differently, there are no definitive answers to these questions. But other people with Alzheimer's have found that engaging in old hobbies like listening to music, dancing or going for a walk helps them take their mind off their troubles.

Loneliness is a common emotion brought on by the disease. You may think that the people around you don't understand what you're going through. It can be comforting to talk to others who have been diagnosed with Alzheimer's disease. That's why support groups are so important. If you don't want to go to a support group in person, consider joining an online discussion group.

You might feel guilty or uncomfortable about asking for help. Let's face it, most of us feel that way whether we have Alzheimer's or not. Losing one's independence is never easy, and we often deny that we need assistance. Because Alzheimer's is a progressive disease, over time you will find it necessary to ask for help more often. Try to accept the help you need. Chances are that others will be pleased to be of service.

ALZHEIMER'S, HEALTH AND SAFETY

ALZHEIMER'S AND YOUR HEALTH

Two of the most important ways to maintain your well-being are to stay healthy and safe. Where your health is concerned it is important that you:

- Rest when you are tired. Try to get six to eight hours of sleep a night and take naps throughout the day if needed.
- Exercise regularly, with your doctor's approval. Make sure not to overexert yourself.
- Eat healthy. Make sure to get lots of fruits and veggies and drink lots of water.
- Cut down on alcohol because it can make your symptoms worse, and don't do any drugs that aren't prescribed by your doctor.
- Take your medications as prescribed, and ask for help if it is difficult to remember when medication should be taken.
- Reduce stress in your daily life as much as possible.

ALZHEIMER'S AND YOUR SAFETY

The gradual loss of your memory can bring new concerns about safety. Difficulties with decision making and communications add to those concerns. Here are some tips to help keep you safe:

- Consider a companion. This can be a friend or a family member, or someone from your church, neighborhood or a local non-profit or volunteer organization. The person you live with may worry about leaving you alone for long periods of time. While you may feel you will be fine alone, having a companion can help the time pass more pleasantly. It can also lessen worry for your loved ones.

- Stop driving when it's no longer safe. Loss of memory can hinder your ability to follow the rules of the road. You may also become less able to judge depth and make quick decisions, and your reaction time will be slower.

- Use alternate means of transportation, like getting rides from friends or family, taking taxi cabs, using public transportation or walking.

- Just as people can wander while walking, they can also become lost when driving or taking a bus, train or airplane. To help protect your safety, enroll in the Medic Alert@+Safe Return program.

- Be mindful of electrical appliances. Leave written reminders to yourself like, "turn off the stove" or "unplug iron." Be sure you have an automatic shut-off feature on the appliances you use most often, especially the ones that can cause harm or fire if left unattended.

- Use smoke detectors and carbon monoxide detectors. Have a friend or relative make sure your detectors are working and that the devices have batteries. Put reminders on your calendar to change the battery.

- Be cautious of people you don't recognize. If someone you don't recognize comes to your door, don't let them in. Instead, write down the person's name and telephone number. You can call a friend or family member you do recognize and trust and have them verify the information at that moment or later, you and a friend or family member can call the person back together.

ALZHEIMER'S AND LIVING ALONE

Many people with Alzheimer's continue to live successfully on their own during the early stages of the disease. Making simple adjustments, taking safety precautions and having the support of others can make things easier. Here are some suggestions for living on your own:

- Talk to the staff at your local Alzheimer's Association office or your doctor about where to go get help for things like housekeeping, meals or transportation.
- Inform your bank if you have difficulty with record-keeping and keeping track of your accounts; they may provide special services for people with Alzheimer's.
- Arrange for direct deposits of checks, such as your retirement pension or Social Security benefits. Try to limit your cash banking transactions.
- Plan for home-delivered meals, if they are available in your community. Check with Meals on Wheels, your local church or ask family members and friends to pitch in.
- Have a family member regularly sort your closet and dresser drawers to make it easier for you to get dressed.
- Leave a set of house keys with a neighbor you trust.
- Schedule family, friends or a community service to make a daily call or visit; keep a list of things you can discuss.
- At some point, it will become too difficult or dangerous for you to live alone. Make plans now for where you will live as the disease progresses.
- You may want to get a helpful roommate, live with relatives or move to a residential care setting.
- Alzheimer's and Your Future
- Because Alzheimer's disease is a progressive illness, the symptoms you are experiencing will gradually worsen. You will need more help. There is no way to predict how or when

this will happen. It is a good idea for you to make decisions about your future as early in the course of the disease as possible.

- Here are some suggestions for future plans:
- Make arrangements at work to cut down your hours, adjust your work schedule or to retire.
- Talk to your employer about Alzheimer's disease and your symptoms, and take someone with you to help you explain and clarify your situation.
- Cut down on your hours or responsibilities if possible.
- If you own your own business, put plans in place for its future operations.
- Consider future living arrangements. Talk to your family or friends about where you want to live, and with whom, to prepare for the time when you will need more care.
- Consider all of the options available, including adult day care programs, in-home care and hospice services.
- Consider naming a person to make health care decisions for you when you are unable to do so. This person should know your wishes about your health care and future living arrangements.
- Make sure your money matters are in the hands of someone you trust, like your spouse, your child or a close friend.
- See a lawyer about naming a person to legally take care of your money matters when you can no longer do it.
- Take someone with you to the lawyer to help explain your situation and to interpret all that the lawyer says.
- Find out about any available options for long-term care insurance.
- Planning ahead assures that your future will be in good hands. It also helps your loved ones make the right decisions for you in the future.

LET'S FIGHT THIS WAR ON ALZHEIMER'S

The greatest cost of Alzheimer's disease is not only financial but personal. This monster of the mind steals our precious memories, memories that comfort us throughout our lives. It steals our independence and finally steals our dignity and gradually wears away the ability to manage the basic tasks of daily life.

Deaths from some cancers and heart disease are declining, while the number of Alzheimer's cases continues to increase every year as the population grows older. If we don't get some control over this disease, it's going to bankrupt both Medicare and Medicaid. When it comes to federal funding for research on prevention and treatment other diseases come out far ahead of Alzheimer's. There is an intense political competition for federal dollars.

Washington has committed $5.5 billion this fiscal year to cancer research, about $1.5 billion to heart disease and $5 billion to research on HIV/AIDS. Research funding for Alzheimer's will reach only about $ 600 million. If you compare Alzheimer's funding to the other major diseases, and compare the spending on research to the cost of care, they are not spending nearly enough to find ways to deal with this problem. It is truly a wonderful thing that the money spent on other diseases have resulted in finding cures and saving lives. We just want to be able to say the same thing one day soon.

There are people trying to find answers on their own every single day. People like you and me, and what I have come up with are things like this:

Coconut Oil – When I gave mom a tablespoon full of coconut oil in her oatmeal every morning, I found that it did help by refocusing her to a point. When I found out about the oil, Mom was in the moderate stage of Alzheimer's. She had been taking the Aricept by this time for about a year. The

Aricept was very helpful; it stopped Mom from repeating her questions over and over. But her alertness was still low. When she had the combination of the coconut oil and the Aricept, there was a noticeable sharpness in my mom. Even though there is an improvement with the Aricept medicine and the coconut oil, time will prove these things only slow the disease down to a point. The decline continues to progress with Alzheimer's.

Turmeric – Turmeric is a golden-colored spice used in curry dishes and is thought to possibly have preventative qualities. There may be something to this because the East Indian people use this seasoning in most of their dishes and they are reported to be the population least likely to get Alzheimer's.

Vitamin D – I have been told that 2000-6000 milligrams of vitamin D per day wards off Alzheimer's. Since a lack of vitamin D can lead to depression, and depression can lead to dementia, then I think taking vitamin D is very important.

Cast Iron – It has been said that the natural iron in the pots is good for our health. There may be something to this. My Aunt Edith, who is my dad's sister, has been using nothing but cast iron pots to cook with her whole life. She just turned 89 this year with the agility and alertness of a twenty-five year old woman. We should avoid using aluminum foil for cooking our foods because the aluminum gets into the food and we digest it. We should not use aluminum foil to store our foods either. The salts and seasonings in the food break down the aluminum therefore causing pieces to get into the food and into our bodies. Our bodies cannot break down aluminum so it floats to the brain and stays there.

There are so many conditions associated to the way we eat these days. It is reported that high blood pressure and cholesterol are factors in getting Alzheimer's. My mother did have high blood pressure and was on the high blood pressure medicine for about 20 years. Alzheimer's is truly a complicated disease because I have spoken with people who have told me that their loved one who had Alzheimer's did not have high blood pressure. So, those who may not have high blood pressure can still get Alzheimer's. This is why the need for a massive government effort to fund research is so critical. We need to know what can cause Alzheimer's, what can prevent it and definitely what can cure it.

We must initiate a global conversation about Alzheimer's disease and other dementias. Despite the prevalence of the disease, it is still widely misunderstood. There is a stigma attached to Alzheimer's and other dementias. People don't want to talk about it. Alzheimer's is now in the same position cancer was many years ago when people would whisper about it; they called it "the big C."

Alzheimer's is a slow-building condition and it can take years or even decades for the protein blockage in the brain to cause diagnosable cognitive problems. We are not terribly good at getting ahead of slow-build conditions. The general sense is yes it is a problem, but we have time to deal with it. Since there are no Alzheimer's survivors so far, then who can campaign for more federal funding? The answer is, those of us who can.

Recently there has been some increase in the federal commitment to Alzheimer's research. Congress created the National Alzheimer's Project the nation's first National Plan to address Alzheimer's disease. They set a target date of 2025 to develop methods of prevention and effective treatment. It has been stated this will take $3 billion annually over the next decade in research funding. But congress to date has never approved more than $600 million in annual funding.

All we know to help ourselves until more is discovered about Alzheimer's, is to do physical exercise which may prevent dementia in old age. Physical exercise seems to increase development of new neurons in the brain. We can eat healthier and worry less to try and prevent depression, because depression can bring on dementia. Most of all we can fight this war which is going to require greater efforts to make Alzheimer's one of the diseases that will become a political favor, and thus have the support of more politicians in Washington.

CPSIA information can be obtained
at www.ICGtesting.com
Printed in the USA
FSHW021826240119
55233FS

9 780977 036134